AROMATHERAPY

A Handbook of Aromatherapy and Essential Oils

(Getting Started Quickly With Aromatherapy and Essential Oils)

Jeffrey Smit

I0135308

Published by Harry Barnes

Jeffrey Smith

All Rights Reserved

Aromatherapy: A Handbook of Aromatherapy and Essential Oils (Getting Started Quickly With Aromatherapy and Essential Oils)

ISBN 978-1-77485-109-8

Legal & Disclaimer

The information contained in this book is not designed to replace or take the place of any form of medicine or professional medical advice. The information in this book has been provided for educational and entertainment purposes only.

The information contained in this book has been compiled from sources deemed reliable, and it is accurate to the best of the Author's knowledge; however, the Author cannot guarantee its accuracy and validity and cannot be held liable for any errors or omissions. Changes are periodically made to this book. You must consult your doctor or get professional medical advice before using any of the suggested remedies, techniques, or information in this book.

Upon using the information contained in this book, you agree to hold harmless the Author from and against any damages, costs, and expenses, including any legal fees potentially resulting from the application of any of the information provided by this guide. This disclaimer applies to any damages or injury caused by the use and application, whether directly or indirectly, of any advice or information presented, whether for breach of contract, tort, negligence, personal injury, criminal intent, or under any other cause of action.

You agree to accept all risks of using the information presented inside this book. You need to consult a professional medical practitioner in order to ensure you are both able and healthy enough to participate in this program.

Table of Contents

Introduction

Did you realize that the human nose can identify and recognize up to 10,000 individual aromas? Our feeling of smell is very strong and it is connected from numerous points of view to different elements of our bodies.

Fragrant healing is the utilization of sweet-smelling and basic oils to keep up and improve the body, psyche, and soul. It is viewed as a comprehensive type of medication that treats the entire individual as opposed to simply the indications of the infection. This reciprocal treatment works with ordinary medication to invigorate the body to recuperate itself.

Plant based treatments have been drilled by individuals around the globe for centuries and have been demonstrated to be powerful all through the ages. Current fragrant healing has based on the revelations of middle age and old sweet-smelling practices to give viable and positive outcomes.

Fragrant healing can be utilized in the home to dispense with or calm numerous basic diseases like colds, hacks, cerebral pains, fevers, muscle hurts and some more. It can likewise raise your degree of protection from sickness and invigorate your body's own safeguard frameworks.

Fundamental oils, when utilized and weakened effectively, are incredibly protected and infrequently produce any symptoms. These delicate and regular enhancements are an extraordinary option in contrast to a portion of the cruel meds of the advanced age. It is not necessarily the case that fragrant healing is a trade for current medication, nonetheless. As a deterrent measure, it very well may be amazingly useful.

This digital book is implied as a prologue to the investigation and practice of fragrance based treatment. All through this book, you will discover plans of basic fundamental oil mixes that you can make to improve your body, brain, soul, and home.

Chapter 1: What Is Aromatherapy?

Aromatherapy means "treatment using scents" and is one of the fastest growing forms of alternative medicine. Aromatherapy is the act of inhaling the scents of essential oils, herbs, or other plant derived scents for therapeutic benefit. Aromatherapy is often used in conjunction with massage or other therapeutic techniques as part of an overall holistic approach at healing and promotion of well-being. Studies show that aromatherapy can be a key player in healing some health problems such as stress and anxiety.

Aromatherapy has been used for centuries in countries such as Japan and China, and is becoming increasingly more popular and well recognized in the United States. Ancient Egyptians used aromatherapy as part of everyday healing, bathing and massage. In some Asian countries, essential oils are pumped into the air ducts of buildings in order to ease the stress level of employees so that productivity increases and also to calm customers so that they are more apt to make a purchase.

Aromatherapy is convenient and can be used anywhere. The oils are easily accessible, and most are relatively inexpensive. The science behind why aromatherapy works is simple – our brains register smells quicker than any other sense. Because of this, our sense of smell dominates all of our other senses and our sense of smell is directly tied to our nervous system. When essential oils are inhaled, they have a direct connection to the part of our brain that controls emotions and memory.

Aromatherapy is becoming more and more popular in the treatment of common ailments. What was once regarded as eccentric and esoteric is now more commonplace and mainstream. Essential oils can be purchased from most major grocery stores and aromatherapy candles, bath additives and oils can be found at most drug stores. The number one use of aromatherapy in the United States is for the management of stress and anxiety. And while little research has been done on the scientific benefits of aromatherapy, lots of independent studies have been done and it is shown that people believe the largest benefit to aromatherapy is that it offers a natural, and most often times organic treatment to an ailment.

Chapter 2: The Basics Of Aromatherapy

Aromatherapy Defined

Aromatherapy, sometimes known as essential oil therapy is the practice of using essential oils to enhance psychological and physical well being. Usually the definition of an essential oil includes all natural, aromatic and volatile plant oils in the different forms that they can come including absolutes, C02s and Hydrosols.However for the purposes of this eBook about how essential oils are used to treat emotional and psychological disorders we are going to mainly be discussing oils that are absolutes or CO_2 created.That is because in these two procedures the oils have been macerated thoroughly by processes that preserve the healing molecules in the oil as best as possible.

For the most part the oils in this book can be either inhaled after being released into the air through a diffusion process or applied to the skin diluted in a carrier oil.Oils that are applied to the skin must be diluted in order to avoid sensitization or irritation to the skin.You can also add essential oils diluted in a carrier oil (such as jojoba, camellia or sweet almond oil) to your bath water and absorb the benefits that way.

However in order for the essential oil therapy to be truly effective in the situation where psychological or emotional well being is the issue it is highly recommended that you use a nebulizer which is a way of cold diffusing the oils through the air so they may be inhaled easily.

When you inhale an essential oil the molecules of the plant extract enter the lungs and then absorbed into the bloodstream where the healing benefits are distributed to the rest of your body.

Not all oils are suitable for both inhalation and absorption. There are direct guidelines in the descriptions of essential oils in this book that can help you determine which ones are likely to cause skin irritation.However you can avoid this risk altogether by inhaling the aroma of the diffused oils instead.

Essential oils are sold in small brown bottle by the ounce.Try to by organic oils where possible, as they are likely to be of a higher quality and also have more of a variety of different healing constituents as part of their chemical make-up.

The goal of getting the benefits of an essential oil is two-fold. Number one it is important to buy the highest quality oil possible that you can afford and number two it is important to be able to distribute that oil through the air as efficiently as possible. There is more information about this later on tis book in the section on diffuserss and nebulizers.

Essential Oils.

Essential oils are also referred to as botanical extracts or essences. Their main characteristic is that they are volatile which means that they evaporate when they are exposed to air. This is not true of "fixed oils" like olive oil that evaporate if the top is left off the bottle.

Essential oil is the fluid extracted from the roots, bark, stems, leaves and flowers of a plant.Oils extracted from these plants come in many colors including clear, red, blue orange, amber, yellow, brown, green and black.Many oils have a slight tinge to them of green, yellow or blue even though they are quite transparent.The color of oil has nothing to do with purity or overall strength or quality.

Although essential oils are highly fragrant they are not the same as a fragrance or perfume which usually is manufactured in a way that dispenses with the healing constituents that are an inherent part of the original distilled or extracted botanical.

Absolutes

Absolute oils are extracted from the plants using hot steam or solvents.Usually distillation or maceration methods are used for essential oil but if the plant is very fragile or deteriorates during these processes then extraction using solvents are used to extract the healing essence. The result is a very high concentration of fragrance that is more potent than steam distilled oils.

Absolutes are a little more concentrated than essential oil.A very small amount of absolute oil can smell very strong and be overwhelming so remember the rule that "less is more" when using these.

Purists in aromatherapy do not recommend using absolutes if possible because sometimes a trace of the solvent used to extract the oil can remain in the oil.Sometimes these solvents are severe carcinogens.

As a general rule it is best avoid using absolutes on your skin simply because they are so strong. Never swallow absolute oil as it could result in poisoning.

CO2 Extracts

Some oils are extracted using a method called CO2 extraction.Carbon dioxide is pressurized until it becomes liquid and is then applied to the plant matter. This acts as a solvent on the botanical matter and the oil dissolves into the CO_2.When the solution is depressurized and the CO_2 evaporates again then what is left is the resulting oil.

This method of extraction often produces much purer thicker oil and it is believed that a lot more of the healing constituents from the original plant are kept when oil is extracted this way.The aromas of these oils also tend to be stronger, more complex and layered so they also tend to be more expensive.

Keep in mind it is not mandatory to buy these more expensive cold-pressed essential oils but it does make them more effective because they are so much stronger.

Hydrosols

Hydrosols might be preferable for you to use in the case of emotional or mental illness as they are very gentle and deliver less of the healing essence to the physical body. This is partly because human skin is much better at absorbing the botanical components using oil as the delivery system.You can diffuse or vaporize hydrosols as well as splash them on their skin but the effect will not be as powerful.

This is because hydrosols are simply the pleasantly scented wastewaters that are left behind after essential oils are extracted from plant matter using steam.Many hydrosols are quite fragrant and do contain some of the healing properties that were in the original essential oils.

They are also sometimes called hydrolats, floral waters or distillate waters.

Hydrosols are much gentler on the skin and do not need to be applied with a carrier oil. They can also be added to the bath directly or used as a cologne or body spray without any danger of sensitization to the skin.

To be most effective however it is recommended that you use CO2 extracts or pure essential oils as they are whole and contain more of the healing constituents needed for you to have an actual impact on your mental or emotional health.

Restoring Sanity:A History of Aromatherapy

It seems that use of aromatherapy for healing of both mind and body has been around for eons. Essential oils have been in use since the beginning of time. Oils are mentioned in Holy books an Ancient Scriptures and have been part of worship in many different religions.Healing with oils is referred to in Buddhist, Christian, Hindu, Jewish and Muslim traditions.

The initial uses of aromatherapy were all about cleansing so that psychological and physical conditions could be healed. This is because even s far back as neolithic times indigenous people burned botanicals ins the form of woods, needles, gums, leaves and plant matter in order to fill a space with healing smoke.Anthropologists believe that the smoke from healing herbs was likely man's first medicines.

Banishing and Summoning Spirits

Essential oils were used for many purposesthroughout history but mostly for summoning or banishing spirits.The wafts of smoke from incense, burning branches and herbal and floral infused steam was thought to create a portal that summoned divine intervention.

One of the most famous examples of oils in the Bible is the bringing of three gifts from the Magi to Baby Jesus in the manger. This is where most of us have initially heard of the essential oils Frankincense and myrrh. The third gift was gold because backs then essential oils were seen as being good as gold they were so prized for their healing abilities. However long before the mention of essential oils in the Bible they were also found in the tomb of King Tut.

In early times it was believed that all kinds of malefic conditions, including emotional disturbances were actually the result of evil spirits, demons and possession. The reason that plant matter was burned was to banish these evil entities that were said to be the root cause of illness.

Records going as far back as 4500 B.C. describe the use of balsamic substances for medical and religious applications. Fragrant oils were used as offering and to anoint sacred objects in temples and sacred spaces in almost every religion.

There is no documented history about when incense first started to appear but it is surmised that it probably appeared a couple One of the oldest books about the use of burning plants for their aroma is dated around 2,700 BC and written by Shen Hung.Plants were burnedto fumigate, purify and elevate the mood and physical outlook of visitors to these sacred spaces.Nowadays you can make your own abode into a sacred space by diffusing aromatic scents through a space in order to change the mood.

The Greeks refined Egyptian methods of healing and distillation.Plants were often burned as fumigations to provide a medicinal benefit. The oils would be inhaled through the smoke, which would then enter the bloodstream. Oils were blended into a fatty base and allowed to melt on the skin.This is often how Myrrh was administered for healing in the days of the Greeks.The Egyptians would also wear solid blocks on essential oil on their heads and allow the oils to drip down their hair and body.The skin would then absorb the oil and it'sbenefits. Myrrh is known for being a pain reliever and mood elevator and is mentioned many times in this book as a way of relieving a number of conditions including depression, grief and emotional pain. In fact, according to the Bible Jesus was offered myrrh in a glass of wine when he was on the cross by Nicodemus.His body was also anointed with myrrh and aloes when it was laid in the tomb.

Hippocrates (400 BC), who is considered to be the Fathered of Modern Day Medicine was the first to study the healing effect of essential oils. He believed that a daily aromatic bath and scented massage with macerated plant matter would keep human beings in excellent health.

During the time of the Roman Empire a book was written called **De Materia Media** that catalogued the healing properties of over 500 plants. It was written by Dioscorides who was a medical practitioner practicing in Nero's army. This was the first encyclopedia of Aromatherapy. However at that time floral waters were used more than essential oils.

From Sacred Rites to Pharmaceuticals

Throughout the Middle Ages essential oils were used for sacred rites, healing and also to banish the new "evil spirits" in people's lives; the viruses associated with the various poxes and plagues that wiped out much of the population every decade.

Essential oils were used for every purpose including the coronation ceremonies of royalty, to seal business dealing and in the initiation of priests.Many of the spices that were used back then are still used for the same purposes todays.The spice trade was an important part of both ancient and medieval economics with Jasmine, Spikenard (the old world name for lavender), roses, Frankincense, Black pepper, Bay Laurel, Cinnamon, Myrrh, Cloves, Cedar wood and Cypress being part of it.All of these essential oils were as prized for their mood balancing and emotional healing qualities as they are today. In fact every single one of these healing herbs is mentioned in this book as being a cure for an emotional disorder.Frankincense was considered to be so valuable that it was actually traded ounce for ounce in gold.

In the Middle Ages technology was invented that will allow for a more efficient cold diffusion of the essential oils. This was a pipe invented by a Persian individual named Avicenna who wrote books about medicine and healing and who was considered to be a polymath in his time. His device allowed for the therapeutic inhalation of the oils so that the patient experienced the maximum effects of the healing constituents.

In the twelfth century a German Abbess named Hildegard grew and distilled lavender for medicinal purposes however what it is most known for, both then and now, was it's ability to heal and calm all kinds of mental and psychological disorders.She even invented a drink called "lavender water" for migraines and sadness that consisted of lavender and brandy.

Lavender was also mentioned often in the Bible where it was referred to as Spikenard.It is the essential oil that Mary used to anoint her hair when we she washed the feet of Jesus.In many households a cross-made out of lavender was hung over the door for protection.

The popularity of this oils eventually led to the development of the pharmaceutical oils that would be used during the evolution of the pharmaceutical industry for the next several hundred years.Many essential oil blends were invented to fight the Black Death during the 14th century.

By the 16th century oils could be purchased at a medieval drug store called an"apothecary.Frankincense, jumper, rosemary, rose and sage were popular oils at the time and are still mainstays when it comes to curing emotional and psychological ailments today.

During the 16th and 17th centuries perfumery came into being and diverged as a separated industry from the creation of essential oils for healing.Although perfumes can be used as a way of uplifting us and reminding us of better times, they are not the same as essential oils that contain particular constituents that directly heal us.

Modern Aromatherapy

Modern aromatherapy began at the turn of the twentieth century when chemical methods of separating the healing constituents in plants were used to make pharmaceutical drugs.

The actual creation of the science of aromatherapy is credited to Rene-Maurice Gattefosse investigated essential oils for use in medicine. In 1928 he burned himself and then plunged his arm into the closet cooling fluid, which happened to be a container of lavender essential oil. The resulting healed quickly and didn't scar.In 1937 he wrote a book called Gattefosse's Aromatherapy , which is still in print and referred to as an essential text.

Many seminal texts on Aromatherapy followed including ones by Jean Valnet, Madam Marguerite Maury and Robert B. Tisserand (who is quoted and cited often in this book.)Tisserand was the first English writer of an aromatherapy book in English. It was called the **Art of Aromatherapy** and published in English. One of the greatest modern students of psychological aromatherapy is Valerie Ann Worwood who wrote the **The Fragrant Mind: Aromatherapy for Persoanlity, Mind, Mood and Emotion** in 1996.This was just at the dawn of the interest in everything New Age including the use of essential oils to heal emotional conditions and alter consciousness.

Unfortunately, during the nineteenth century, pharmaceutical and cosmetic companies to lower the cost of manufacturing them copied essences chemically. This resulted in the loss of their therapeutic properties.This is why it might be a good idea to buy organic oils or at the very least read your labels very carefully to make sure you are not buying a chemical replica of the real thing.

Today aromatherapy is more respected than ever as a proven and legitimate way of addressing and healing all kinds of conditions, including the emotional conditions that are discussed in this book. No matter what the specific intention of using the oil is it tends to relieve pain, improve mood and promote a sense of well being and relaxation.

Chapter 3: Asthmas And General Disposition

Now that we have given out some advice regarding the situation with bronchitis and other throat and lung diseases, it is time to talk about some more general-use oils. Or any infection or general disposition you may try oils such as Cedarwood, Cypress, Eucalyptus, Elemi, Helichrysum, Lemon, Pine needle, Myrrh, Myrtle, Orange or Thyme. Most of those are still very useful when it comes to lung problems. No matter the situation, whenever you are inhaling or rubbing any of those oils it is important to stay warm and to get a lot of rest. The effect may not only be lost if you immediately go back into the cold or start being too active, but it may even worsen your situation.

Basic aromatherapy, of course, is not that serious since it is usually done for general comfort. Putting some scented candles around the room is always nice for the mood and it can have a twofold effects during the cold season, keeping your breathing easier.

However, if you are having real trouble breathing the best advice, again, would be to go to the doctor. In the mean time you can use Cypress as quite the effective method for slowing down your coughing, especially if you are going out.

When it comes to asthma on the other hand, the list is pretty long. Cypress is useful in that regard as well, but you could better try Lemon, Sweet Marjoram, Rose Otto, Rosemary or Tea tree. You can take some of these ails and make a blend for asthma attacks.

As you can see some of the suggestions are the same and repeat for the different symptoms. This is because most of those oils have multiple purposes and that is exactly what makes them such a popular method of alternative medicine. Usually it doesn't matter which combinations of oils you use, but try not to blend more than five or six oils at once.It is bet to start small, trying out the effects of only one or two oils. Before you start blending left and right make sure that you are not allergic to any of the ingredients.

Something that you can try for improving your breathing would be an inhalation of diffusion blend. You are going to need twenty five drops of Myrtle, ten drops of Thyme, ten drops of Eucalyptus radiate and ten drops of Niaouli. Once you blend those you can put around ten drops from the mixture in a bowl of preheated water and let the vapors go in the air. It would help if you try to breathe slowly and deeply, while keeping yourself warm.

If you are using this recipe with a child do not cover their head with a towel. It is enough to sit around the bowl and inhale deeply. You can also put some of the mixture on a personal inhaler but mind the portion – it shouldn't be too much.

As an alternative variant you can put three or five drops of carrier oil and massage the mix on the chest and the back. Since the oils have an antibacterial and antiviral effect they are great for threating germs and improving the general health condition of the person that is being treated.

Chapter 4: Aromatherapy Do's And Don'ts

Dabbling into the wonderful world of essential oils can be an incredible experience. But of course, before you start on your personal aromatherapy journey, you need to know the basic do's and don'ts. Here are a few tops that every beginner should know about using essential oils.

Do: inform yourself as much as you can about aromatherapy. Read articles, watch videos, listen to podcasts, and buy more books if you have to. While buying your first set of essential oils is pretty easy, you need to know about any possible safety issues you might encounter along the way.

Don't: think that perfume or fragrance oils are the same thing as essential oils.

Perfume oils are usually synthetically made so they don't have an therapeutic benefit to offer.

Do: choose a reputable source for your essential oils. The quality of essential oils varies greatly from one company to another. It's also worth knowing if the oils are pure or if they're diluted with a carrier oil.

Don't: be afraid to reach out to companies to ask them any questions about the essential oils or products that they carry. Most companies are usually more than happy to help out.

Do: aside from the common name, make the effort to know the botanical names of the essential oils that you plan to buy. Bay essential oil for example can refer to two different oils because they can come from two different plants.

Don't: just buy your essential oils off the street. While street fairs and craft shows may offer an extensive line of aromatherapy products at a fraction of the cost, you'll have a hard time going after them later on.

Do: know the country of origin of the essential oil you want to buy. Choose essential oils that were sourced from plants that are organic and / or ethically farmed.

Don't: buy your essential oils from just one company. Don't hesitate to shop around and compare products from different sources.

Do: look for a wholesaler source for essential oils and aromatherapy products if you're planning to buy in bulk. The quality of oils varies from store to store and company to company so again, don't just settle for one brand.

Don't: store your essential oils in clear bottles that are exposed to sunlight. For oils to last, make sure that you store them in amber bottles placed in a cool, dark area in your home.

Do: keep yourself updated on safety information of different essential oils. If you're suffering from a medical condition or taking any prescriptions, make sure to ask your healthcare professional if it's safe for you to use aromatherapy. Pregnant women should take extra caution, especially if they're at that stage that they're sensitive to scent.

Don't: apply pure essential oils to skin without first diluting them with a carrier oil. Some essential oils are so potent that they can be very irritating to skin. In extreme cases, some can even cause skin to burn or scar.

Do: the most important thing that you need to remember is keep an open mind. While it's crucial that you take every safety precaution there is, it's also important that you see the learning process as something that's fun and exciting.

Chapter 5: Improved Mood

Have you ever had a bad day when you woke up grumpy or sad and all this evil ended up affecting your whole day? Or maybe somebody gave you some bad news and your bad mood ended up dragging on for the rest of the day? Anyway, it's hard to get out of a bad mood when that mood appears. The oils, in those moments, can help a lot.

There are several oils that you can use to make you more excited. Remember, always use quality oils that have not been tampered with.

Marjoram

Marjoram is a herb that you can have in your spice drawer. Known for its delicate taste, marjoram is related to oregano, but it is sweeter. The Latin name for marjoram is **Origanum Marjorana**. The plant oil is extracted by steam distillation. Marjoram helps to improve your mood with its warm scent.

To use marjoram, place one or two drops in a little carrier oil and massage the soles of your feet.

Vetiver

Vetiver oil, or **Vetiveria zizanoides**, has an earthy and balsamic aroma. Vetiver is also known as Bunchgrass, Khus or Ruh Khus. This herb has its oil extracted through steam distillation. If you're feeling overwhelmed or distracted, this is the oil for you. If you feel lonely, this oil can also help.

To use, put a drop in your hands, rub and bring it to your nose. Breathe for a minute.

Lemon

What do you remember about lemon? You'll see? Lemon cake? Lemon oil, or **Citrus x limon**, is an oil that provides joy. If you're feeling tired, oppressed or angry, lemon can cheer you up and calm you down. The lemon oil is extracted through the peel. The lemon has a fruity and citrus aroma.

To use lemon, drip up to ten drops into a diffuser where you can inhale.

Balance Hormones

Have you ever been upset or angry with the world and don't know why? Have you ever had premenstrual syndrome or attacked everyone when you were on PMS? These are signs that your hormones are unbalanced. If you're always cold, your thyroid may be out of balance. Always warm? Could be overproduction of

39

hormones. Other glands in your body may not be producing enough hormones, while others may be producing too much.

There are several oils that you can use to balance hormones, check out the main ones here:

Ylang Ylang

Ylang Ylang, or **Cananga odorata**, is an oil that you may have heard of as an aphrodisiac...

Anyway, Ylang Ylang is a powerful oil in the hormonal balance. It can be used especially for women who suffer from menstrual acne. Ylang Ylang is distilled in cycles. Different stages carry different therapeutic compounds of the plant in the oil. These fractions of oil are collected in the same way as olive oil, the first being the best, the second the second the best and so on. Ylang Ylang is a tree and its flowers are harvested for oil distillation.

To use the Ylang Ylang, spread four to six drops in a diffuser.

Clary Sage

Clary Sage is an oil that is also known as **Clary** or **Clear Eye**. This herb has a musky smell and is considered of utmost importance in hormone control. It grows like a very tall plant, reaching a height of 2 to 4 meters. Flowers with a variety of purple flowers. Clary sage is steam distilled. Men, you may want to skip this next part, but women, you'll want to read this. Clary is perfect for PMS and during menstruation. It contains phytoestrogens, also known as food estrogens. These phytoestrogens regulate hormones by protecting the uterus from various types of cancer. That means less colic and less PMS symptoms!

To use, add up to six drops to a carrier oil and massage the lower part of the belly. You can also diffuse up to six drops in your diffuser.

Myrtle

Myrtle, or Myrtus communis is a bush, although it is probably not the same as what you can see blooming in the garden. The myrtle has a history of being used to balance hormones. The oil is extracted by steam distillation of flowers, stems, leaves and fruits. Myrtle oil balances the thyroid gland and ovaries. It has been studied to balance cases of hypothyroidism.

To use the myrtle, make a massage oil with coconut oil, or with your favorite carrier oil, and five drops of myrtle. Massage the rib, back, abdomen, legs or feet.

Improved Sleep Quality

Have you ever been up all night? You wake up tired, like you've never slept enough? Do you feel like you're never rested? Believe it or not, aromatherapy can help you with all these problems.

If you belong to a large percentage of people who suffer from insomnia, be aware of these tips. There are several oils that you can use to improve the quality of sleep. Remember, always use quality oils that have not been adulterated, especially if used orally. Never forget to look for therapeutic grade oils.

Lavender

The name itself makes you want to fall asleep, doesn't it? Also known as **Lavandula angustifolia**, lavender is great for relaxation and sleep. The lavender oil is distilled by steam from the floral buds. The smell is floral and sweet.

To use lavender oil as aromatherapy, place up to six drops in your diffuser. You can also add a little rose oil. If you have an automatic diffuser that will turn off when you are out of water, let it run while you fall asleep. You can also add up to four drops of lavender to your favorite carrier oil to use it in a relaxing massage.

Roman Chamomile

Roman chamomile, or Chamaemelum nobile, is a refreshing oil that will allow you to relax and relax. It can be used to relieve tired mind and body. Roman chamomile oil is distilled by steam from the plant's flowers.

To use, place up to five drops of oil in your favorite carrier oil and give a relaxing massage. You can also add two drops to your bath.

Valerian

Valerian, or **Valerian officinalis**, is a unique plant. Along with its ability to calm down, it has the ability to relax. Another fact that makes valerian oil so unique is how it is distilled. This herb does not have its oil distilled from its leaves or flowers. The oil is extracted from its root. Valerian improves the quality of sleep, so if you're one of those types of people who don't sleep well, it might help you.

To use Valerian, add two drops to your favorite carrier oil and apply to the bottom of your feet.

Promoting Healing

Scratches, broken bones and bruises, in short, all these misfortunes are things that can happen in life. Some oils promote recovery caused by these accidents, killing bacteria and starting cell growth, others heal bruises and reduce scars. Some also cure urinary tract infections, fungal infections, and athlete's foot. When it comes to fungi, viruses or bacterial infections, aromatherapy and essential oils can be of great value.

Incense

One of the three gifts the wise men brought to Jesus was incense. It has been used by the ancients even before Bible times. There are three types; sacred incense (**Boswellia sacra**), Serrata incense (**Boswellia serrata**) and Frankincense Carterii (**Boswellia carterii**). Each one of these incense has its own importance. Some believe that Sacra and Carterii are essentially the same because the seed looks the same. But they are grown in different geographical areas and on different soils. When plants sprout, they look very different. Both promote healthy skin growth and aid in bruising. Sacred incense is currently being studied as a treatment against cancer. It has been shown to decrease tumors and cancers.

To use any of the Incense, dilute one to three drops with a carrier oil and use topically.

Melaleuca

Melaleuca is also known as **Tea Tree Oil** or **Niaouli**. In fact, these two oils present themselves as Melaleuca in their botanical names, but the similarities stop there. **Tea Tree Oil** is known as **Melaleuca alternifólia** and is a stronger version of Melaleuca and should not be used on sensitive skin unless it is highly diluted. Niaouli, or **Melaleuca quinquenervia**, is a sweeter smelling version of Melaleuca. It is strong too, but it is safer to use on sensitive skin when diluted correctly. Both oils kill bacteria and fungi and promote skin growth. Melaleuca is steam distilled from the leaves of the plant.

To use any of Melaleuca's oils, dilute one drop every six drops of sesame oil or another of your favorite carrier oils. Apply topically to the wounds. You can also add two drops to a "scald feet" to kill the fungus.

Myrrh

Another of the three gifts brought to Jesus, Myrrh, is considered a healing oil. It comes from the resin of a small, thorny tree and is steam distilled from the resin. The oil is thick and can be applied like incense. Myrrh is a powerful antimicrobial. It kills fungi, bacteria and viruses and promotes healthy skin growth.

To use myrrh, put a drop in some of your favorite carrier oil and use topically.

Pain Relief

You've certainly hit your pinkie at the door or the foot of the bed, twisted your ankle, or had chronic back pain. Fortunately, there are several oils that can be used to relieve your pain.

Remember, always use quality oils that have not been adulterated, especially if you are using them orally. Look for therapeutic grade oils.

Wintergreen

Wintergreen, or **Gaultheria procumbens**, is a shrub that looks a little holly, but much smaller. It has small green leaves and red fruits. The leaves are harvested and the oil is made from steam distillation. Wintergreen oil has a fresh, minty smell. To use Wintergreen oil, add three drops of oil with a small amount of oil from your favorite carrier. Rub on any part of the body that is sore. The oil can be used on sore necks, knees and elbows. It's great for people who deal with rheumatoid arthritis. Wintergreen cannot be swallowed and care must be taken when using it on sensitive skin.

Copaíba

Copaíba is a powerful oil to relieve pain. Copaíba, or **Copaifera officinalis**, comes from a tree that grows in the Amazon forest. To produce the oil, a hole is drilled in the trunk of the tree. This resin is used for steam distillation. Copaíba is great for any pain and suffering. If you suffer from arthritis, weather-related pain, fibromyalgia, sciatica, painful or broken limbs, this oil will be able to help you.

To use Copaíba, use five or six drops on your diffuser or add two drops to a small amount of your favorite carrier oil. You can also put a drop or two in a capsule and take it orally.

Carnation

Cravo, or **Syzygium aromaticum**, is a traditional remedy for toothache and sore throat. It acts with an anesthetic effect on the area where the pain is emerging. Cloves are flower buds that form the cloves' tree. The oil is made by steam distillation. He tastes spicy and spicy. It should only be taken for a maximum of two weeks.

To use carnation oil, add a drop of carnation oil to a small amount of coconut oil and apply to the source of your pain.

Chapter 6: The A-Z Of Essential Oils

Essential One-Stop Aromatherapy Chart - Essential Oils

					sinus, bronchitis, catarrh, arthritis, rheumatism, circulation, gingivitis
Sage	herb	leaves/flower	China, Mediterranean region	astringent	
Sandalwood	tree	bark	India, Indonesia	sedative, anti-fungal, antibacterial	catarrh, menstrual issues, cystitis, scars, skin infections
Spearmint	herb	leaves/flower	United States, Europe, Mediterranean region, parts of Europe	digestive	flatulence, nausea, colic, indigestion, intestinal cramps, fever
Tea Tree	tree	leaves/twigs	Australia	anti-inflammatory, antibacterial, antifungal, antiviral	cold sores, burns, colds, bacterial and viral infections, warts, thrush, acne, bronchitis
Thyme	herb	flower	Egypt, Mediterranean region	stimulant, general tonic	rheumatism, lethargy, bacterial and urinary tract, wounds
Ylang-ylang	tree	flower	Indonesia, Philippines, Comoro Islands	sedative, general tonic	high blood pressure, anxiety, depression

NAME	TYPE	DERIVED FROM	PLACES OF ORIGIN	POWER IN OIL	USE IN THERAPY
Almond	herb	seed	India, Indonesia, South America	digestive	cough, hoarseness, infections
Bay	tree	leaves	West Indies, South America	antiviral	cold, flu, sprains, psoriasis
Bergamot	tree	peel	Morocco, Italy	antidepressant	cough, colds, fever, acne, wounds, eczema
Chamomile	herb	leaves/flower	England, France, Hungary, Bulgaria	anti-inflammation	inflammation, acne, eczema, psoriasis, menstrual issues, dermatitis, migraine, burns
Cinnamon	tree	leaves/twigs	India, Sri Lanka	antiviral	stimulation, cold, cough, circulation
Clary Sage	herb	flower	France, Spain	sedative	sore throat, depression, depression

Carrier Oils

Aromatherapy is at its most effective when the essential oils you use are in their purest state. This pure state of the plant material's essence is also highly concentrated - most essential oils are deemed unsafe for use in their raw state.

53

To prepare them for the body, you dilute the oil with a base that will help spread the oil's properties evenly without lessening its potency. The perfect base for this purpose is provided by carrier oils.

Carrier oils or base oils (named for their function), are nothing but pure oils derived from sources in nature, such as nuts, seeds and vegetables, that contain a fatty base. These oils on their won are of high nutritious value. Most of them contain a host of vitamins, such as A, D and E that help maintain excellent skin, nail and hair health. They also contain essential minerals such as calcium, phosphorus, iron, manganese etc, along with healthy fats such as Omega-3 and Omega-6. All these nutrients combine to make carrier oils excellent tools to blend your essential oils with.

In addition, carrier oils generally have a more viscous and thicker texture than the light essential oils. This makes it easy for the essential oil to reach large areas of skin with the same tiny amount and potency. Carrier oils are also less volatile than essential oils, which means that they do not evaporate as easily when in contact with air or heat. Due to this characteristic, they are excellent tools to make your essential oils last longer.

The best ways means of extracting your carrier oils is either through the methods of maceration or cold pressing. Sources for carrier oils are also generally higher-yielding than essential oil sources. This means that you will get more oil from five pounds of olive than you would from five pounds of lavender. It is, however, cheaper and far more convenient to purchase your carrier oils from your local health stores.

When you purchase your carrier oils, ensure that they are extracted through natural means, and not manufactured through synthetic means. Common carrier oils such as olive, coconut and vegetable oil are also used for culinary means. These cooking oils may not have been extracted through a natural source, and will be ineffective in aromatherapy. Try and source your oils from a reputed health store in your area or even online.

Nearly all carrier oils will keep for a long time if stored in a cool and dry area. Since these oils are thicker in texture, you may find that some carrier oils develop a cloudy appearance and firmer texture at low temperatures. This is nothing to worry about; the oils retain their clear, liquid state when the temperature is warmer. The following are a list of the most commonly available carrier oils, with their benefits as well as uses.

Essential One-Stop Aromatherapy Chart - Carrier Oils

NAME	DERIVED FROM	COLOR	USAGE IN BLENDS	RICH IS	USE IN THERAPY
Sweet Almond	kernel	pale yellow	used undiluted	vitamins, minerals, proteins, glutosides	dermal itching dryness, soreness, inflammation, all skin types
Apricot Kernel	kernel	pale yellow	used undiluted	vitamins, minerals	dermal sensitive, dryness, inflammation, aging
Avocado	fruit	darkgreen	10% dilution	vitamins, proteins, fatty acids, lecithin	dermal dehydration, dryness, eczema, all skin types
Borage seed	seed	pale yellow	10% dilution	vitamins, minerals, gamma linolenic acid	aging, psoriasis, eczema, pre-menstrual trauma, menopause, cradle troubles, cell regenerator, all skin types
Carrot	root	orange	10% dilution	vitamins, minerals, beta-carotene	aging, psoriasis, eczema, itching, dryness, scarring, rejuvenating

D'astre	seed	yellow	20% dilution	vitamins, minerals	dermal itching, dryness, soreness, inflammation, all skin types
Corn	kernel	pale yellow	used undiluted	vitamins, minerals, proteins	all skin types, soothing
Evening Primrose	flower	pale yellow	10% dilution	vitamins, minerals, gamma linolenic acid	aging, psoriasis, eczema, pre-menstrual trauma, menopause, cradle troubles, cell regeneration, all skin types
Grapeseed	seed	colorless pale green	used undiluted	vitamins, minerals, proteins	all skin types, soothing
Hazelnut	kernel	yellow	used undiluted	vitamins, minerals, proteins	all skin types, slight astringent
Jojoba	bean	yellow	10% dilution	minerals, proteins, collagen protein	psoriasis, eczema, acne, hair fall, penetrating, all skin types
Olive	fruit	green	20% dilution	vitamins, minerals, proteins	rheumatism, hair care, homemade cosmetics, soothing
Peanut	seed	pale yellow	used undiluted	vitamins, minerals	all skin types

Safflower	flower	pale yellow	used undiluted	vitamins, minerals, proteins	all skin types
Sesame	seed	dark yellow	used undiluted	vitamins, minerals, proteins, amino acids, lecithin	rheumatism, psoriasis, eczema, arthritis, all skin types
Soya Bean	bean	pale yellow	used undiluted	vitamins, minerals, proteins	all skin types
Sunflower	flower	pale yellow	used undiluted	vitamins, minerals, proteins	all skin types
Wheatgerm	kernel	pale yellow	10% dilution	vitamins, minerals, proteins	all skin types

57

Chapter 7: How Does It Work?

There are individual components that work with essential oils that will immediately boost and affect your mood.

But the question still lingers, how does this all work?

The components within the essential oil penetrate the skin, and thereby open up the blood vessels. When doing so, you are essentially relieving any pain and swelling that may be apparent, which will bring healing to the area and stimulate blood flow.

This will in turn be able to have an effect on your entire body, including the brain, organs, and nervous system. This means there are a lot of variables that you can explore, depending on what type of essential oils you are using as well as what type of effect you want to have on the body.

There are a few things to take into consideration when you are learning about how they work and are preparing to use them in your personal life.

Safety Concerns

The following are some safety concerns you should pay extra attention to.

Dosage

There are certain essential oils that are known to be toxic that are largely dependent on dosage.

This is an important feature of essential oils, as some essential oils may have too high of a concentration or be used in the wrong doses. When done so, you run the risk of developing tumors or can develop other symptoms that are unhealthy.

They may also be damaging to internal organs such as the liver or kidneys, and if not careful may be damaging to the skin.

Purity

When you are altering essential oils with other synthetic materials, you run the risk of completely altering the chemical compound and morphing it into something that will not be agreeable to your body.

Sometimes essential oils are cut with cheaper synthetic substances, or even with vegetable oil. In order to avoid altering your chemical compound in a way you are not prepared for, check the label.

The label should be completely honest if bought from a reputable source. If there is a label that includes a portion of vegetable oil, that is not necessarily a bad thing.

At times, pure essential oils are outrageously expensive, such as 100 dollars for a teaspoon of rosebud essential oils. This dilution may be relevant in order to make the essential oils available on the market.

Application Method

Depending on your essential oil, determine what the safest method for applying is.

Some essential oils are ok to be inhaled, while others can be applied to the skin.

This variation is not constant and will be largely dependent on which oils you are interested in using.

Do your research before using the preferred method of essential oils to make your safest choice.

Getting Started

If you are a novice to using essential oils, but you are not sure with how to start, take the next basics into consideration for getting started.

Sauna

This is a great place to start using essential oils. You can add essential oils to the water and throw it on the heat source.

A little bit goes a long way, so 2 drops is sufficient for 600 ml of water. Best to inhale include: rose, geranium, ylang ylang- best to avoid in a sauna: eucalyptus, lemon, peppermint, and pine.

The former have sweeter and more subtle attributes while the latter is more astringent and harder to inhale.

Cold & Hot Compresses

This is especially great for strained muscles, bruises, or other forms of pain.

Compresses help reduce pain that can be used all over the body, and can even help with congestion and problems with internal organs.

Take a clean cloth or bandage and soak with a mixture of essential oil that is mixed with water. Next, put it over the affected area.

This is a low maintenance way of protective and healing your body.

Vaporizations

Heat the oil until it is released and evaporated into the air.

This will prove to be a therapeutic practice, and depending on which essential oils you use, will help create a mood that will have great, lasting effects if used consistently.

Never use essential oils directly on a hot light bulb, however, and make sure your heat source is well attended.

Using Essential Oils

For this section, we'll focus on the most common uses of essential oils:

Skin & Face

Hair Care

Stress Relief/ Anxiety

Improved Sleep/ Mood

Skin & Face

Here are 5 types of essential oils that will help with your skin care regime.

Geranium Essential Oil:

Geranium oil is great for aging or dry skin. It has balanced and nurturing qualities that will help with maintenance, but can also help with burns, eczema, and lice.

This is also known to be emotionally uplifting and can be bought at a great cost.

Lavender Essential Oil:

While this oil is gentle to use, it also has a great impact. This is particularly great for skin types that tend to be sensitive to varying types of skin.

Use liberally for acne, athlete's foot, burns, psoriasis, ringworm, or insect bites. It is gentle but strong, and available in a low price range.

Patchouli Essential Oil:

This type of oil has an earthy quality to it and is great for oily skin. It is used to eliminate dandruff, eczema, or oily hair.

This is a safe essential oil as long as it is diluted and is very easy and affordable to obtain.

Rose Essential Oil:

It has a great fragrance and is great to use during pregnancy. It can be healing for veins and dry/aging skin.

Violet Essential Oil:

This is in a slightly higher price range, but is a great healer and is specifically used to heal inflammation and thread veins.

It can open pores and blackheads, and is ideal to use in vaporizers.

Hair Care

Many hair care regimes take a lot of synthetic materials.

Take for instance shampoo- shampoo is filled with additives that can have negative effects such as rashes, dry skin, and skin irritation. Check your labels and try to replace some synthetic materials with natural essential oils.

Here is a general list of what essential oils to look for depending on your hair type.

For Normal Hair:

Neither greasy nor dry, no coloration, and is usually shiny.

Lavender Essential Oil

Rosemary Essential Oil

Lemon Essential Oil

Geranium Essential Oil

Cedarwood Essential Oil

These oils help keep your hair looking healthy and feeling great.

For Dry Hair:

Tends to look dull, tangles easily, and is prone to split ends.

Lavender Essential Oil

Rosemary Essential Oil

Sandalwood Essential Oil

Geranium Essential Oil

These oils are designed to add life and replenish dry hair.

For Oily Hair:

Lavender Essential Oil

Rosemary Essential Oil

Lemon Essential Oil

Peppermint Essential Oil

Cypress Essential Oils

These oils will help reduce the appearance of oily hair.

To Treat Dandruff:

Rosemary Essential Oil

Lemon Essential Oil

Lavender Essential Oil

Thyme Essential Oil

Basil Essential Oil

Cypress Essential Oil

Sage Essential Oil

These oils will help relieve the effects of itchy, dry scalp that is caused by dandruff.

Stress Relief/ Anxiety

Here is a list of the top essential oils used to relieve stress and anxiety.

Lavender: Known as "universal oil", has calming and balancing properties.

Frankincense: Has a great exotic and warm aroma. It is commonly used for stress relief, but has healing properties as well.

Rose: Another highly versatile oil. Provides relief from stress and depression.

Chamomile: Excels in treatment of irritated skin, yet also helps reduce anxiety, paranoia, and hostility.

Improved Sleep/ Mood

Here is a list of common essential oils used to help improve your sleep patterns or uplift your mood.

Lavender Essential Oil

Valerian Essential Oil

Roman Chamomile Essential Oil

Sandalwood Essential Oil

Marjoram Essential Oil

Chapter 8: Benefits Of Aromatherapy

As mentioned earlier, the fragrance of essential oil is not just valuable for relaxing massages in the spa or making our home smell nice. You will be surprised to know that aromatherapy can be used to treat a range of common health complaints ranging from anxiety to stiff muscles, high cholesterol to insomnia, and depression to chronic arthritis pain. People are going back to aromatherapy – a method used by their ancestors for thousands of years.

Yes, even you can use essential oils at home and see a significant improvement in your quality of life. Generally, the easiest way to use aromatic oils at home is to have a diffuser installed. Remember, scents can trigger different emotions and psychological effects in different people.

So, for a change, think about the many scents you are exposed to throughout the day. Some fragrances are soothing and create positive moods and thoughts in your mind. Ask any person if they've ever smelled roses and jasmine randomly and felt happier. This means that aromatherapy can easily be integrated into your life. After all, your nose is quite used to doing all the work on a daily basis.

On a serious note, all you have to do now is choose the specific fragrances that will help you achieve your goals for mind and body wellness. Bring these oils home and let your brain and nose do the rest.

The Many Uses of Aromatherapy

Aromatherapy can be used everywhere from spas to hospitals and homes to offices. Historically, essential oils have been used to improve mood and relieve pain. In fact, essential oils from bergamot, lemon, sandalwood, lavender, rose, and orange have shown promising results if you talk about relieving stress, anxiety, and depression.

Essential Oils and Pregnancy

There is clinical evidence that essential oils, mainly lavender and rose, were used by midwives to help ease delivery anxiety in pregnant women. Many expecting moms felt less need for pain medication when essential oils were used during labor. The practice continues even today. However, do consult your healthcare provider for more information related to use of essential oils during delivery.

Aromatherapy and other Medical Conditions

Massage with essential oils can be quite helpful for people with depression. The benefits are thought to be related to relaxation caused by the scents.

Oil obtained from fennel and aniseed may help relieve painful symptoms of menopause and premenstrual syndrome.

Other medical conditions that can be alleviated from aromatherapy include:

Hair loss or alopecia

Anxiety

Constipation

Insomnia

Muscle and joint pain associated with rheumatoid arthritis and cancer

Itching

Psoriasis

There are Just So Many Scents!

The amazing ability of aromatic oils will surely tempt you to bring some home, but which oils should you use? If you want to use aromatherapy, it can be a daunting task to figure out the scents you need to use and why. There are many scents, but as mentioned earlier, not all oils are beneficial for all purposes.

Here's some guidance to help you select the right essential oils for a few common complaints. Don't forget to consult your healthcare provider just to check if these oils are right for you. Remember, the scents listed here may not show immediate effects in your case since every person is different. Our bodies react differently, and you may be required to stick to the new regimen for a few days in order to see the desired beneficial effects.

Oils Helpful for Fatigue:

Some useful essential oils mentioned here are discussed in more detail in section five.

·Basil

·Cedar wood

·Clove

·Eucalyptus,

·Jasmine

·Lemon

·Neroli

·Peppermint

·Vanilla

Oils Helpful for Headaches:

·Basil

·Chamomile

·Cinnamon

·Ginger

·Eucalyptus

·Lavender

·Lemon grass

·Peppermint

·Thyme

Oils Helpful for Anxiety:

·Lavender

·Chamomile

·Rose

·Vanilla

·Myrrh

·Bergamot

·Cardamom

·Neroli

·Orange Oils Helpful for Sinus Congestion:

·Basil

·Cedar wood

·Clove

·Eucalyptus

·Fennel

·Rosemary

·Tea TreeOils Helpful for Depression:

·Lemon

·Neroli

·Peppermint

·Rosemary

·Sandalwood

·Bergamot

·Cedar wood

·Jasmine

·Lavender

Oils Helpful for Indigestion:

·Lavender

·Lemon grass

·Orange

·Peppermint

·Rose

·Rosemary

·Sandalwood

·Thyme

·Anise

·Fennel

·Basil

Oils Helpful for Menstrual Cramps:

·Basil

·Chamomile

·Ginger

·Lavender

·Rose

·Rosemary

·Sage

Oils Helpful for Muscle Stiffness and Soreness of Joints:

·Chamomile

·Eucalyptus

·Lemon grass

·Rosemary

·Sandalwood

·Myrtle

These are a few examples of fragrances or essential oils that may help improve your health and relieve pain. You may also seek help from a reputable aromatherapist if you're not sure about the oils you need to pick.

A qualified aromatherapy expert can also guide you about the various aromatherapy options that are available as well as supportive diet and lifestyle changes that can help achieve an optimal healing outcome.

Mental Health Benefits of Aromatherapy

Your brain, without a doubt, is the most important part of your body. And if anything goes wrong with your brain, your overall physical and emotional well-being can be badly affected.

As discussed in the overview, stress is one big problem that affects us. Not only does stress have a negative impact on your sleeping pattern and behavior, but it also weakens your immune system. This is why people are more prone to medical complications and all kinds of diseases when they are stressed out.

As we have seen quite a few health benefits of aromatherapy, it is wise to see how essential oils can help you deal with emotional problems. That's right. These oils, when inhaled and applied on the skin, trigger different reactions in your brain. You may find that negative emotions and stress simply vanish after you inhale these naturally occurring magical molecules.

Every part of your brain has a specific function. For example, there's a special part that controls your heart rate and breathing. Similarly, there's another part of your brain that plays an important role in maintaining your balance. In addition to physical and physiological functions, your brain is also responsible for controlling your emotional state.

Anger is Really Bad for You!

Anger seldom has a good outcome. If you let your emotions get the best of you, not only do you suffer, but those around you suffer as well. Therefore, it's best to keep anger at bay and stay calm, even in a frustrating situation.If you're having problems keeping cool, you can use jasmine or orange oil to tame your temper without much effort.

Want to Overcome Grief?

Sadly, we all go through a rough phase in our lives, a time when we are emotionally devastated. The death of a loved one or any other depressive event may leave you stricken with grief, but you can use aromatherapy to lift your spirit. Those of you who are having a tough time dealing with grief can seek help from geranium and lavender oil.

Why So Anxious?

Sometimes you just cannot keep calm and you don't really know what's bothering you. To let go of the worries in life, you need to first regain your focus and concentration. And this is exactly what bergamot and clary sage can help you achieve. So, if you're feeling anxious, do give these oils a try, and your brain will thank you for it.

Say Goodbye to Bad Memory

The simplest way to improve your memory and concentration is to use cypress and peppermint oil. If you cannot focus on important tasks, it's not a bad idea to use a few drops of basil oil.

You can allow the aroma of these therapeutic oils to diffuse evenly in your room to experience the beneficial effects. As mentioned earlier, you can consult a qualified aromatherapy expert to guide you with the application methods. More details on application methods are coming up later in the book.

Aromatherapy and Stress Management

Stress, which is now a normal part of our lives, is definitely not an exhilarating experience. The negative emotions inside you badly affect your confidence and self-esteem. The effects of stress are quite obvious. Your body experiences stiff muscles, mouth ulcers, and fatigue, among many other problems derived by stress.

Sadly, there are a number of psychological and emotional side effects as well. You may feel an increased desire to abuse unhealthy stimulants, such as alcohol, tobacco, and coffee. You may also feel a lack of confidence, frustration, and low self-esteem. If left untreated, negative emotions and stress tend to build up and slow down your body's functions and weaken your immune system.

Aromatherapy directly acts on your hypothalamus, a specific area in your brain that triggers the "fight or flight" response. The use of aromas influences your physiological functions, and you begin to think more clearly.

Most aromatherapists prefer using two or more oils for successful stress management. Recommended oils include geranium oil, which helps regulate hormonal imbalance. Jasmine, rose, and neroli are effective to relieve depression, and stimulating citrus oils help uplift the mood.

Essential oils are usually applied by means of a relaxing body massage as a part of stress management. A mildly refreshing and revitalizing body massage produces beneficial physical and psychological effects that tend to remain for much longer. Some aromatherapists also use essential oils in a warm bath to produce the desired physiological and emotional effects.

Chapter 9: Actions Of Essential Oils

Which essential oils have antibacterial properties?

In 2000 The Journal for Microbial Chemotherapy published a paper of their findings of essential oils and their antibacterial properties. A total of 14 oils were tested in petri dishes to assess their reactions in the fight against bacterial infections. The various strains of Staphylococcus , influenza and E Coli were all exposed to the rigours in turn of Cinnamon Bark, Lemongrass, Perilla, Thyme (wild) , Thyme (red),Thyme (geraniol) ,Peppermint , Tea tree,Coriander,Lavender (spike),Lavender (true),Rosemary,Eucalyptus (radiata), and Lemon oils.

Across the board, all of them showed some degree of anti bacterial activity, but by far the most effective were cinnamon bark, Red and Wild Thyme and Lemongrass which inhabited every one of the six different strains tested. Tea tree also fared extremely well in the fight against E Coli. The two oils which showed the least activity in the strains were lemon and Eucalyptus radiata.

To the list of essential oils I would recommend for antibacterial properties Manuka, Niaouli, Ravensara and also Oregano.

Most of the oils on the list exhibit some degree of capability for dermal irritancy so I would always recommend dilution for these. The very best carrier to fight off in faction will be a very light lotion with the oils mixed in a dilution of around 1% essential oils and 99% carrier. A small amount applied regularly to the inside of the arm will start to fight off infection very quickly.

These oils would also work very well as a cleaning agent for surfaces to rid the home of germs too.

Which essential oils are adrenal stimulating?

One of the key problems in managing stress is that over time our adrenal glands become exhausted from all of the external pressures stimulating them for an extended amount of time. Essential oils can help here.

In the fight against stress, rather than finding oils which will stimulate the adrenals, we want ones which will boost them. I will explain why.

The adrenals are small glands which sit at atop our kidneys. Their job is to secrete a variety of different hormones. The one which we are primarily concerned with here is adrenaline. This hormone is what gives us our edge and keeps us safe in times of danger. It rules what is called our "fight and flight" syndrome.

This raises our heart rate and breathing and fills our muscles with oxygen to strengthen them in the fight we see before us. Now in the times of our ancestors this was very useful because it allowed us to outrun the sabre tooth tiger, slay it and eat it.

When the feasting was over, he slept and the adrenaline levels could return to their resting levels. Today however we live under so many pressures the levels never quite return to normal. This over stimulation is what makes us feel burned out.

The oils which support the adrenal glands are Mandarin and Camomile maroc. These help to strengthen the adrenals and allow them to begin working effectively again.

The adrenals work in tandem with other glands in the endocrine system, (mainly the pituitary gland) and also the liver.

Oils which help to support the liver are rosemary, peppermint and eucalyptus. The pituitary should be supported using nutmeg oil.

I would advocate a blend of oils in a home treatment cream or lotion which can be applied very regularly, perhaps as often as three times a day on the inside of the arm. This gives the opportunity of the essential oils to stimulate the healing mechanisms which will very quickly have the adrenals functioning effectively.

Which essential oils act as vasodilators?

Vasodilator essential oils work in a very similar way to a very rigorous exercise work out. They encourage the blood vessels to open much wider so the blood becomes engorged with oxygen. This has two main effects. The skin then takes on a very healthy plumped up appearance but it also brings about this wonderful feeling of wellness a bit like the runners high.

There are three essential oils which act as true vasodilators and these are marjoram, geranium and also ylang ylang oils. Geranium can also be very effectively used for reducing the amount of redness in the cheeks which comes from rosacea for the same reason. Ylang ylang is able to reduce blood pressure too through its vasodilatory expression.

Complementary oils to add to blends are lemon, myrtle, cypress, black pepper and lemongrass. All of these will stimulate circulation and encourage good supply.

The best methods of application will be different according to the effects you want to bring. Most people would want good muscle strength. For this it would be best to utilise the benefits of a massage. The kneading and pummelling will add to the oxygenation of the muscles and further enhance their effects. The oil drop to the bath water too would be very effective. I would not use black pepper, lemongrass or lemon in this way as they are a little harsh on the skin. Cypress may be a little too invigorating before bed but geranium, ylang, ylang, myrtle and marjoram will also have the added benefits of bringing excellent sleep

For rosacea, add to your daily moisturiser. As many applications of ylang ylang as you can find will help lower blood pressure, blend it into massage oils, creams and lotions and also drip it into the bath.

Aromatherapy for the Body

Does aromatherapy calm and relax the body?

People potentially use aromatherapy for its ability to relax and calm more than for any other reason. The essential oils are able to do a very good job alone but when mixed with the soothing strokes of a massage, it can become absolutely sedative bliss.

The body is a complex machine taking directions entirely from the brain. Essential oils are able to absorb through the skin and into the blood stream and work in a way that allows the body to let go of tension and begin to relax.

First we need to look at what causes tension in the body which is usually the effects of stress. When we feel under pressure or experience anxiety or fear, our bodies secrete a hormone called adrenaline. This causes our heart rates to go faster and our breathing to speed up too.You may recognise how we clench the muscles in our shoulders and fists in particular but also our legs and buttocks too (mainly because of a natural response for the body to want to run away from the situation).

When a muscle has been over worked for a period of time it can no longer manage the bi product lactic acid which is left behind. Over time it becomes crystallised and gets knotted into the muscle fibres. Perhaps you have felt this giveaway crunching when you roll your neck?

Essential oils such as lavender and camomile are very soothing not only to the muscles but also to our frazzled nerves. Marjoram sends out messages right across the central nervous system for the organs to calm down.

Juniper is extremely good at breaking down the toxicity which is left in the joints and muscles leaving them clean and refreshed. The muscles fibres are then able to slip across each other easily making movement far less painful and easier.

Many people like to use aromatherapy oils in the bath to relax the body too. This is an excellent way to get them into the blood stream quickly. The water relaxes the muscles and opens the pores. It also gives a very large surface area into which the oils can absorb. This is both extremely relaxing to the body and calming to the mind.

Which aromatherapy oil is the best to use for massage to alleviate body pain?

Pain in the body can come from a variety of sources and aromatherapy oils can help reduce the agony you feel. By far the most effective pain killers you can find are lavender and camomile oils. Lavender you can use neat on the body and camomile must be diluted.

Often pain in the body will come from a build up of toxicity which the body has not been able to rid itself of. This could come from over exertion in exercise or from the physical effects of stress for example. These toxins will eventually turn crystalline making it more difficult for the fibres to slip over each other easily. This friction causes pain. Juniper oil is wonderful for braking down this toxicity and flushing it out of the body.

Similarly the pain may result from nerve pain, headache, toothache or sciatica perhaps. Use of rosemary reduces the surges of agony this can produce and alleviates pain.

Care must however be taken with use of rosemary as it is high in neurotoxins which are able to induce fitting in people who are sufferers of epilepsy.

Tendons which have become stressed and torn over time can find help from frankincense oil. It restores elasticity to the fibres and helps them to regain strength.

All of these essential oils work well when dropped into the bath at the end of a long day. About 5 drops is plenty enough to fill the bath water. Massage too can be very helpful as the muscles are kneaded and warmed to stimulate them too.

Blend around 5 drops of oil into a 10 ml of carrier oil to create a blend. Carrier oils can be any vegetable oil that you find in your kitchen cupboard but very effective ones are calendula or borage.

Any good aromatherapy recipes for physical wellness?

(Amounts are numbers of drops to use)

Aphrodisiac massage oil – Jasmine x 2, ylang ylang x 2, Sandalwood x 2 in 25 ml of carrier oil

For nerve pain – Rosemary – Frankincense x 2 Rosemary x1 Lavender x 3 blended into 25ml of body lotion

To use for muscle training- Cedarwood atlas x 2, black pepper x1, Juniper x 3 in 25 mml of body lotion

To alleviate bugs and germs – Tea tree x 2, Manuka x1, Kanuka x 2, Ravensara x 1, Niaouli x 1 and Elemi x1 mixed into 25 ml of body lotion and applied often as you remember on the inside of the arm.

Aromatherapy for the Mind

How does aromatherapy affect the person's mood?

Aromatherapy works on two very different systems within the body. Essential oils have the ability to absorb through the skin and into the blood stream. Once there they circulate around the blood stream and travel to the places which need them.

They can also be taken to the brain via the sinuses; that is they can be inhaled. For the most part oils will be inhaled because they are in evaporator or perhaps in a bath but the heat allows the oils to turn to gas and travel up the patient's nose. This is a very fast journey as the sinuses are the only nerves which go directly to the brain.

Scientific trials have recently proved that essential oils have the ability to cross the blood brain barrier and when their molecules reach the brain they affect an area called the limbic system. This is the part of our brain which not only governs our emotions but our memory too. With this is mind it can be that a memory from long ago can be triggered by a simple smell from the past.

The chemical constituents of an oil vary from plant to plant. Oils which contain components called sesqiterpenes have the ability to uplift the mood, while those containing esters (like camomile, and valerian for instance) are more likely to sedate.

Used in massage too the effects are further enhanced by the warming and relaxing of the muscles. The process of being touched is very nurturing and can promote a feeling of deep well being.

Which aromatherapy oil is the best for treating anxiety?

Long term anxiety can be detrimental to health. Using aromatherapy not only eases the mind but also reduces the physical after effects which can result on the body.

Geranium oil is the powerhouse when treating anxiety. Best used 5 drops in warm bathwater it quickly helps to lift the anxiety away.

Frankincense is a very ancient oil which has been used since time immemorial to induce a meditative state. It slows down the breath which in turn allows all of the other body processes to follow suit. It is relaxing to the muscles and very sedative too.

Lavender is soothing and a relatively cheap oil to buy. Apart from relaxing the mind and body it will also aid restful sleep.

The deep and musky tones of vertivert and patchouli make them wonderfully soothing oils. They will both calm the mind and also release tension from the muscles.

There are times though when anxiety can come from a short sharp shock and that can really induce panic. A drop of camphor really helps to alleviate trauma. It is a very strong oil and should be used with care, one drop in any treatment and no more.

Massage is by far the most effective method of using aromatherapy to treat anxiety. The actual process of doing nothing for an hour and a half is really quite difficult to do. It is the admission to yourself that the world won't just stop if you do. This is extremely conducive to healing.

Touch is a very soothing thing too and while the therapist kneads your muscles and calms away your stress the essential oils can set to healing your mind and body too.

How can aromatherapy fight off depression?

Aromatherapy uses the concentrated essences of plants to bring about changes in the mind and the body. Essential oils are one of the only things known be able to cross the blood brain barrier. Once there they are able work on a part of the mind called the limbic system. This controls not only our emotions but also our memory too.

Depression has many different symptoms and while aromatherapy can certainly help to alleviate these, medical guidance from your doctor should be sought. Here are some ideas of oils which will help.

Use uplifting oils to help to improve your mind. Oils such are **bergamot, geranium, melissa and cypress** are all wonderful for moving the gloom.

Research has shown that the amount of light we get on a daily basis affects not only our moods but our physical body too.A gland called the pineal is responsible for manufacturing hormones melatonin, which regulates sleep, and also serotonin, which affects mood, learning, intimacy and also many of our digestive process. If you find you feel withdrawn or unable to connect emotionally this could be a source of your problems. This particularly is true of people suffering from Seasonal Affective Disorder. Incidentally we know that women are more than 70% more likely to suffer from this condition and to suffer connected symptoms. Oils which can help boost your pineal are: **Lavender, Sandalwood, Frankincense, Parsley and Pine.**

Anxiety and hopelessness are best treated by the doctor especially if they present on a longer term basis. **Geranium and rose** are helpful as well as **mandarin and myrtle** oils. **Clary sage** is incredibly sedative and allows you to distance yourself emotionally from the problems. Use this oil with care; be aware that it does not mix well with alcohol as it can cause delusion.

Chapter 10: Essential Oil Blends

Essential oils are powerful when taken at face value, but combining them will place even more powerful concoctions at your fingertips. It only takes a minute or two to create an oil blend and you're able to combine the effects of a number of oils into a single potent blend. It's important to carefully consider the oils you're adding to an oil blend because it's all too easy to combine oils and end up with a blend that has properties you didn't want to add.

Here are the steps I recommend when deciding which oils you'd like to blend together:

Look for essential oils that have the properties you desire. For example, if you have a cold, you're going to want to look for oils that have decongestant and expectorant properties. If your body aches all over, you're also going to need oils that work for aches and pains. Antiviral and antibacterial oils can help ease the duration of the cold, especially if used early on, so add those to the list as well. Got a headache? Add oils that eliminate headaches to the list, too. Once you've got a list of oils you're considering and their properties, move onto step 2.

Look for the oils that cover a number of the problems you're trying to solve. If you're only trying to solve one problem, look for oils that work best to eliminate or ease that problem. These should be your top contenders.

Look at the other properties of the oils and eliminate oils that have undesirable effects. For example, if you're looking for oils that help ease the effects of the cold, but it's getting late at night and you're ready for bed, you'll want to eliminate oils that have a stimulant effect because they might keep you awake. If you're pregnant or trying to get pregnant, oils that have emmenagogue properties should be crossed off the list. Other considerations that need to be made is possible interactions with medications you're taking and the effect the oil is going to have based on your current medical condition.

Consider how the remaining oils are going to smell when combined. This is one of the tougher things for beginners to take in because there's a lot to consider. More on this in a bit.

Combine the essential oils. If you're creating a new oil blend, you can combine a few drops of each of the oils to test them out. Make sure you keep track of what you've added to the oil blend or you run the risk of creating a blend you love, but aren't able to replicate. If you're creating a blend you're already familiar with, you can combine more oil, so you'll have it available when you want it.

Place them into an airtight glass container and let them sit overnight. This is the hardest part. Don't judge your oil blend right away because the oils need time to meld together and mature. Wait a day or two before smelling your blend and deciding whether you like it or not.

Not too bad, right? Blending essential oils is easy when all you're concerned with are the therapeutic benefits of the oils. It gets much more complicated when you start worrying about the fragrance of the oil blend in addition to the benefits.

Categories and Notes: Creating Fragrant Oil Blends

While you could simply blend essential oils based on their therapeutic properties alone and end up with oil blends that smell halfway decent and work well, it's preferable that you have at least a passing knowledge of how the fragrances are going to combine with one another. This will allow you to look at the essential oils you're considering using and decide which of the oils will probably combine the best. Keep in mind that much of what you're going to learn in this chapter boils down to personal preference, so it's going to take some experimentation on your part to decide what sort of oil blends you like the best.

It's part science, part art and a whole lot of experimentation. Take the time to learn the ins and outs of blending fragrances and you'll be able to come up with oil blends that are amazing.

There are three key considerations that must be made when creating essential oil blends:

The effect of the oil.

The category the oil falls into.

The note of the oil.

We already discussed looking at the effect of the oil in the previous chapter. Once you've determined which essential oils best suit your needs, it's time to start looking at how the different oils will combine and that's determined by the category and the note.

The category of the oil is the grouping into which an essential oil is placed based on a decision made by looking at both the type of plant the oil came from and the fragrance the oil has. Here are the categories essential oils are divided into:

Campherous oils. Campherous oils like eucalyptus and tea tree oil have the medicinal fragrance of camphor. They're strong oils that can easily overpower lighter oils in a blend if you aren't careful.

Citrus oils. These oils have the light smell of citrus. They include orange, bergamot, lime, grapefruit and lemon essential oil.

Floral oils. Floral oils are derived from flowers and smell like the flowers they were distilled from. Popular floral oils include geranium, rose and lavender oil.

Herb oils. These oils are taken from and smell like the herbs that are used for cooking and include popular herbs like basil, oregano and rosemary.

Mint oils. These oils have the unmistakable fragrance of mint. Spearmint and peppermint are two of the more common mint oils.

Spice oils. These oils are referred to as Oriental or exotic oils in some literature. They have unmistakable fragrances that are unlike any other essential oil. Oils like patchouli and ylang ylang oil are classified as spice oils.

Wood oils. These oils are taken from trees. They smell fresh and woodsy and sometimes feature a campherous fragrance. Pine, cedarwood and eucalyptus oil are all tree oils.

Blending oils based on the category they're in is more art than it is science, so you can place oils in the different categories based on the fragrance you detect when you smell them. As you can see, there is some overlap between the groupings. For example, eucalyptus oil could be classified as either wood oil, because it's taken from trees, or campherous oil because of its fragrance. I would personally place it into the campherous category, but a pretty good argument could be made that it's a wood oil.

Here are some basic rules to follow when blending essential oils:

Wood oils can be blended with most other oils to good effect.

Campherous oils are tough to blend with other oils because they tend to overpower oil blends. If you do decide to blend them, use small amounts of the campherous oil and larger amounts of the other oils.

Floral oils combine well with spice oils and citrus oils. **They also work well with some wood oils.**

Citrus oils can be used to add the light fragrance of citrus to most oil blends, but they tend to work best with floral oils or herb oils.

Mint oils blend well with citrus oils, but can quickly overpower a blend.

Of course, you know what they say about rules—they were made to be broken. Some of my favorite oils blends ignore the previous rules altogether and came about as a result of me thinking, "I wonder what would happen if I blended [oil A] with [oil B]." It doesn't always work, but as long as you only blend small amounts of oil, your experimental blends won't be too expensive and you can either use them quickly or throw them out.

The next consideration that must be made is the note of the oil, which is a classification of the oil based on how long the fragrance of the oil lasts. There are three basic notes:

Base notes. These are the heaviest fragrances and they stick around the longest. Base notes are notes you'll still smell hours after application. Spice oils and some wood oils are classified as base notes.

Middle notes. Heavy notes, but not quite as heavy as base notes. They're the bridge between the top notes and the base notes. All of the categories contain at least a few oils that are classified as middle notes.

Top notes. These are the first notes you smell in an oil blend. Top notes are light, and they dance around your nose and quickly dissipate. Top notes are scattered throughout the categories. Most of the citrus oils are considered top notes.

The way notes work is the first fragrance you smell in a blend is the top note combined with the other notes. It's a light note that quickly dissipates, leaving you with the middle and base notes. The middle note is often the defining note of a blend because it provides the bridge between the top note and the base note. Once the middle note has dissipated, you're left with the base note, which can last a long time after you apply an oil blend.

Don't forget to factor in the smell of any carrier oils you plan on using. Most carrier oils won't add a lot of fragrance, but they may add a slight nutty or fruity aroma to the mix.

Essential Oil Blends to Try

Blending essential oils is fun, but when first starting out it can be a bit daunting. The oil blends in this section are all designed to get you off to a good start, but aren't the end-all, be-all of essential oil blending. Use them as they are or feel free to modify them to suit your tastes. These blends use only the 10 oils from the "Stocking Up" chapter to create a number of effects. When you think about it, it's amazing how versatile essential oils really are.

These recipes are all best-suited for diffusion or being diluted and applied topically. They might work in candles, bath bombs, skin care products and for other applications, but they haven't been tested.

I used parts as the unit of measurement for the recipes. In order to use the recipes, all you have to do is substitute

The Cold Buster

1 part peppermint oil + 2 parts lavender oil + 1 part eucalyptus oil

If you're congested or feeling stuffed up, a few whiffs of this oil blend might be all it takes to ease the symptoms of your cold or seasonal allergies. This oil blend works best when you add it to a sink full of hot water and inhale the steam. It can also be diluted with carrier oil and rubbed onto your chest, but it might get a little warm!

The Floral Happiness Blend

1 part geranium oil + 1 part lavender oil + 1 part German chamomile

This blend will leave rooms it's diffused into smelling like a flower garden. What more could you want?

The Good Morning Blend

2 parts lemon oil + 1 part peppermint oil

If you've got a long day ahead and want to start it off right, this is a great oil blend to diffuse into the kitchen while you have breakfast. You'll feel wide awake and alert after a few minutes.

Fresh Air

1 part lavender oil + 1 part lemon oil + 1 part oregano oil

This blend takes 3 essential oils that can be used on their own to freshen the air in a room and combines them to create a great-smelling blend that will eliminate even the toughest of odors. Diffuse it into a room or add it to a spray bottle full of water and mist it on items you want to destink.

Detox

1 part geranium oil + 1 part peppermint oil + 1 part citronella oil

The Detox blend works on multiple levels. It aids the digestive systems and helps the body eliminate toxins. It can be added to a bath you're soaking in or it can be diluted and applied topically.

The Bug Blaster

1 part peppermint oil + 1 part citronella oil + 1 part eucalyptus oil

This blend is hell on wheels when it comes to eliminating bugs, but I've got to warn you. It's extremely potent and must be diluted heavily prior to topical application. Even then, you might not be able to tolerate it.

The Back to Earth Blend

1 part frankincense oil + 1 part German chamomile oil

When you're wound up and your emotions are on the verge of getting the best of you, the Back to Earth blend is a grounding blend that will help you corral your emotions. Turn down the lights, sit down and breathe deeply while you diffuse it into the room.

Fever Buster

1 part lemon oil + 1 part lavender oil + 1 part peppermint oil

Dilute this oil and apply it to the forehead, back and neck for fever relief. It should only be used with minor fevers. Bad fevers or fevers that don't let up within a day or two require medical attention.

Anti-Aging Blend

2 parts frankincense oil + 1 part geranium oil

The regenerative properties of both of these oils can be combined to tighten up aging skin and to help reduce wrinkles and skin damage.

The Cleansing Blend

2 parts lemon oil + 1 part citronella oil

Combine these two oils and add them to a spray bottle full of water to create an oil blend that can be used to clean all sorts of hard surfaces. This blend can also be diffused to cleanse the mind and the body.

Aches & Pains

2 parts peppermint essential oil and 1 part German chamomile

Dilute this oil blend with carrier oil and massage it into aching muscles or joints. The analgesic properties will help deaden the area and will provide temporary relief from the pain.

Burns & Wounds

2 parts lavender oil and 1 part tea tree oil

Add this blend to lukewarm water and use it to wash out minor wounds. It can be applied to the bandage prior to covering a wound to promote healing and help prevent scarring.

Chapter 11: Other Essential Oil Recipes

Rosemary And Peppermint Lip Balm

Ingredients

8 spoons of cocoa butter

12 spoons of Beeswax

28 drops of Peppermint essential oil

12 drops of Rosemary essential oil

16 drops of Vitamin E oil

Method

Heat a saucepan. Add the beeswax, cocoa butter and Vitamin E oil to it. Allow the mixture to melt and combine well.

Remove the saucepan from the heat. Allow the mixture to cool completely.

Pour the Rosemary oil into the saucepan next.

Add the Peppermint oil next and mix well.

Whip up the mixture till it reaches a smooth consistency. Store it in a clean container.

This refreshing lip balm can take care of your chapped lips!

Peppermint Mouthwash

Ingredients

1 1/3 cups of Aloe Vera juice

1 cup of water

4 teaspoons Baking soda

48 drops of Peppermint oil

4 teaspoons of Witch Hazel

Method

Take a bowl. Add the Aloe Vera juice and Witch Hazel to it. Pour in the water and mix it well.

Add the baking soda into the bowl slowly. Mix it.

Then add the peppermint oil to the bowl next.

Mix until all the ingredients blend well.

Store the mixture in a clean container and keep it in a cool and dark place. Use it daily for better results.

Vanilla Hand Soap

Ingredients

8 bars of Castile soap

12 litres of water

40 drops of Vanilla extract oil

Method

Take a saucepan. Pour some water into it and heat it.

Take one soap bar first. Grate it over the water. Repeat the same with the other bars.

Let the grated soap melt and blend in the warm water.

Remove the pan from the heat.

Allow the mixture to cool down completely.

Add the vanilla extract oil to the saucepan next.

Mix all the ingredients well. Allow it to set.

Headache Mixture

Ingredients:

- 28 drops Basil

- 28 drops Rosemary oil

- 320 ml sweet Almond oil

- 56 drops Lavender oil

Method:

Take a small and dark glass vial.

Use a clean cloth to clean the glass vial. Let it dry completely.

Add the ingredients into the vial one by one.

Shake the vial well. This is to ensure that all the ingredients are mixed well.

Get rid of stress by applying this mixture on your forehead. This combination has a soothing effect on the nerves. It can take care of your headaches.

Sandal Oil Mixture

Ingredients:

- 4 to 8 drops of sandalwood essential Oil

- 4 drops of honey

- 4 to 8 drops of virgin olive oil

- 2 glasses soy milk – unsweetened

Method:

Take a small and dark glass vial.

Use a clean cloth to clean the glass vial. Let it dry completely.

Add the ingredients into the vial one by one.

Shake the vial well. This is to ensure that all the ingredients are mixed well.

A sip of this mixture would put an end to your craving for sweets.

Minty Magic

Ingredients:

- 100 drops of peppermint oil

- 8 to 16 drops of Spearmint oil

- 8 to 16 drops of ylang ylang essential oil

- 4 tablespoons of sea salt

Method:

Take a small and dark glass vial.

Use a clean cloth to clean the glass vial. Let it dry completely.

Add the ingredients into the vial one by one.

Shake the vial well. This is to ensure that all the ingredients are mixed well.

Say no to indigestion problems by sniffing this mixture as and when required!

Organic Oil Mixture

Ingredients:

- 80 drops of basil oil

- 80 drops of marjoram oil

- 8 drops of oregano oil

- 8 drops of thyme essential oil

- 4 tablespoons of sea salt

Method:

Take a small and dark glass vial.

Use a clean cloth to clean the glass vial. Let it dry completely.

Add the ingredients into the vial one by one.

Shake the vial well. This is to ensure that all the ingredients are mixed well.

Inhale this mixture to curb your hunger pangs. Your digestion power is also improved by inhaling this mixture.

Sandalwood And Rose Perfume

Ingredients

80 drops of sandalwood oil

4 tablespoons of Jojoba oil

20 drops of Rose oil

Method

Take a small bowl. Pour all the oils into it and mix well.

Store the essential oils mixture in an airtight container.

Apply a little of the perfume after bath.

Ensure that you do not apply too much of it as both Rose oil and Sandalwood oil have strong fragrances.

Chapter 12: Choosing Your Carrier Oils

The variety of carrier oils available for you to choose from as a newbie in the science of aromatherapy can get you a little bit confused at first; however, don't worry because this book will cover that.

Choosing your carrier oils is not too different from choosing your essential oils-you simply choose carrier oil that has all the properties you desire and can provide you with all the benefits you want from aromatherapy.

This means you must arm yourself with basic information about the carrier oil and its properties to help you know if it is ideal for what you wish to achieve using aromatherapy. Some properties you need to look out for include the action and viscosity of the carrier oils. You can experiment with different blends until you find a blend that suits your specific needs. This is one of the most important keys to succeeding with aromatherapy and getting the most satisfactory results. We will talk about synergy in aromatherapy later, which will focus on blending different oils to get a blend that provides more enhanced benefits.

Below are some common carrier oils used in Aromatherapy

Almond Oil

This carrier oil is perfect for dry, irritated and aging skin. It has very soothing, nourishing and skin reconditioning effects and is believed to be high in Vitamin D, proteins and GLA acids.

Apricot Kernel Oil

This carrier oil is excellent for all skin types including. It is high in vitamins A, C and E. Its light texture makes it easily absorbed into the skin.

Arnica Infused Oil

This is simply olive oil infused with Arnica. It is traditionally used as an herbal remedy for bruises, inflammation, and joint pains. It is known to act fast and gets absorbed into the skin fast. However, it is advised you do not apply it to open wounds.

Avocado Oil

This carrier oil is excellent for sensitive, irritated skin as well as for treating skin conditions such as severely dry or aged skin, psoriasis and eczema. It is deeply nourishing and soothing as well. This carrier oil contains Vitamins A, B1, B2, D and E. It also contains amino acids, panthethenic acid, lecithin, and several other essential fatty acids.

Borage Seed Oil

This carrier oil is good for aging, sunburned and damaged skin. It is one of the widely known sources of essential fatty acids, vitamins and minerals. It is good for relieving pains and excellent for supporting the mobility of tissues and joints.

There are several other carrier oils such as Coconut oil, evening primrose, GrapeSeed oil, Kukuinut oil, Jojoba oil, Neem oil, Ricebran oil, Rosehip oil, Sunflower oil, St. Johns Wort oil, Comfrey Infused Oil, Rosemary Infused Oil, Sea Buckthorn Oil, etc.

Let us look at some ideas of using carrier oil

Some ideas on how to use your carrier oil in aromatherapy

Sweet Almond, Apricot and Peach are very versatile and can be used for both facial treatments and body massages since they are easily absorbed because of their very light viscosity. If you are allergic to nuts, sunflower should be a good alternative.

Borage, Evening Primrose, Black seed, Rosehip and Jojoba oils all deliver very impressive results when used in facial aromatherapy treatments, but for body massages, you need to dilute them with much lighter oils.

Wheatgerm and unrefined Avocado are excellent for nourishing your skin when used as an overnight aromatherapeutic treatment. However, they are a bit too heavy to be used for body massages. They also have very strong odor, which some people find a bit offensive. If you can ignore their offensive odors, you can be sure to enjoy their rich nutrients and essential fatty acids that help keep your skin soft.

Let's see synergy in aromatherapy:

Synergy In Aromatherapy

Every essential oil used in aromatherapy is already a synergy of different natural ingredients with specific healing properties. This explains why aromatherapy is so effective for the treatment and cure of different ailments using these wonder oils from plants.

Each of these oils is made up of several chemical compounds; one of nature's numerous wonders one can't fathom in all totality. A single plant can contain specific compounds in different parts like the roots, stem, leaves, flower, fruits, which when combined can become a very potent formula for the cure of a myriad of diseases.

The complex structure of the chemical compounds contained in essential oils derived from plants is the reason why one essential oil can have multiple healing benefits. For instance, peppermint oil helps treat nervous, skin, hepatic, immune, circulatory, psychological and intestinal disorders.

However, the use of chemical substances such as pesticides, herbicides, germicides and chemical fertilizers can lead to loss of some of the rich phyto-chemical compounds contained in these essential oils from plant species, thereby decreasing their healing effects. This explains the need to synergize some of these oils once their components, properties and benefits are known to increase diversity in unity. Combining some of these oils to meet a specific need help create more potent complex formulae without upsetting the natural balance.

Blending tips you may find useful:

Blend different oils known to cure a particular disease for enhanced effect

Blend oils from different parts of the same plant

Blend oils that contain same active ingredients

Blend oils with same biochemical make up.

Aromatherapy Blends For Taking Care of Different Ailments

We already talked about synergy and how blending different essential oils can help you produce more impressive and lasting results. When it comes to blending your carrier oil and essential oils to meet different needs, your choice of carrier or essential oil will be determined by what health condition you are trying to manage. For every 1 fl.ounce carrier oil, add 10-12 drops of essential oils. Make sure you refer to the list of oils we mentioned eailer and choose oils that complement each other.

Blends

For stress

6 drops of Clary Sage

2 drops of Lemon

3 drops of Lavender

For improved sleep

5 drops of Lavender

5 drops of Roman Chamomile

Relief for sore muscle**s**

4 drops peppermint

2 drops of Ginger

1 drop of Black pepper

5 drops of Eucalyptus

Sex drive blend

8 drops of Sandalwood

2 drops of Jasmine

To Use

Mix the oils thoroughly and store in an airtight, dark glass container. Use ½-1 teaspoon for massage.

Aromatherapy Massage To Relieve Stress, Tension And Feel More Relaxed

The aromatherapy massage technique below can be used by anyone at home, in the work place or anywhere else. If you are using these steps at home on someone or you get someone to use them on you while at home, any flat, clean, uncluttered surface can work well as a massage table. Simply lie down or get your subject to lie face down.

Select and apply a suitable blend of essential oil and carrier oil.

Start from the legs with strokes delivered with flat palms moving in long, smooth motions starting from the ankle down to the knees or all the way up to the hip region. This helps spread the oil evenly and warms the tissues. Follow this by working on tight areas around your leg.

Repeat the same massage strokes on the back on both sides of the spine, covering the entire back region. After warming up the back tissues, use the fingers, wrists, knuckles and sometimes elbows to work more deeply on the tissues. Tight muscles can be relieved by working locally in the tight areas with firm and gentle strokes.

The arms and hands can be worked on while you or your subject lies either face down or face up. The same strokes and movements used on the legs and back region are to be repeated until all tensed muscles have been worked on and relieved of tension.

The remaining part of the massage can be done while your subject lies face down. Reach under the neck to comb your fingers upward from the back up to the base of the skull. If the patient is lying face down, allow the weight of his neck to indicate the amount of pressure you need to apply with your fingers so as not to apply too much pressure, to avoid muscle cramping or injury because of the awkward angle of the hands. Moderate intense stroking movements can be used across the top of the shoulders because that region is more prone to muscle tension. Stroke the upper chest area making sure you avoid the throat area.

For the facial area, use flat palms in gentle upward motion to stroke over the head as a way of relaxing the face. To release tensions, make gentle circular strokes from the forehead going all the way down to the chin. Use your knuckles to massage the subject's jaw line. This can be done by stroking small, light friction circles that begin from the cheeks and move outwards to the jaw joints. The light circles can equally move up to the ears and behind the ears. As the strokes gently progress to the temple region, lighter pressure should be applied. Use the pads of your thumbs to smoothen the forehead starting from between the eyebrows, while stroking in outward motion as you move to the temples.

Massage the feet last in order not to introduce bacteria from the feet to other parts of the body. You can start the feet massage from the ankles and go across the top of the foot towards the toe area with gentle strokes and moderate pressures. Roll each toe between the fingers and tug gently. Apply circular friction to the soles of the feet and heels using your thumb pads. Make sure you wash your hands after foot massages.

Chapter 13: Recipes For Health And Well Being

Aromatherapy Cure for Insomnia

It should be understood that essential oils in aromatherapy are not medicinal cures or remedies for insomnia. Rather, they have the ability to have a relaxing and calming effect on one's mood and body to help a person fall asleep easier and faster. People with serious sleep disorders are advised to consult a doctor for the appropriate treatment.

For an aromatherapy formula that will help put you to sleep, you will need ten drops of Roman Chamomile, five drops of Clary sage, and five drops of Bergamot. Blend these essential oils together and store in a glass bottle, preferably one with a darker color. Place a drop or two in a piece of tissue paper and place the tissue paper inside your pillow case before going to sleep.

You may also opt to use a diffuser blend by making a blend with the ratio of two drops Roman Chamomile to a drop of Clary Sage and a drop of Bergamot. Lavender can provide relaxation, but can have the opposite effect when excessive.

Four Aromatherapy Massage Oil Recipes

Aromatherapy is popular in massage as most essential oils help the body to relax and reduce stress. To create the perfect aromatherapy oil for massage, you will need a fluid ounce of carrier oil.Sweet almond oil is recommended. Mix the carrier oil with the essential oil or essential oil blend and store in an airtight container, preferably in a dark container.

Recommended essential oils can vary depending on the goal of the massage. If the massage is for reducing stress, the ideal essential oil is a blend of six drops of Clary Sage, two drops of Lemon, and three drops of Lavender. If the massage is intended to be an aphrodisiac to heighten the passion, a blend of eight drops of sandalwood and two drops of jasmine is recommended. If it is intended to be a sleep-inducing massage, put ten drops of Roman Chamomile. If you wish to alleviate soreness in muscles, the ideal mix is composed of two drops of ginger, a drop of black pepper, four drops of peppermint and five drops of eucalyptus.

To use in the massage, only half to a full teaspoon is needed for each massage.

Aromatherapy Cure for Menstrual Cramps

Periods can be the most uncomfortable and excruciating time of the month when experiencing unbearable menstrual cramps. This recipe will help you alleviate the cramps if applied through a gentle massage over the abdominal area.

You will need a glass bottle, preferably a dark-colored one for storing purposes. For the ingredients, you will need a fluid ounce of Jojoba, five drops of Peppermint Essential Oils, four drops of Cypress Essential Oils, and three drops of Lavender. Mix oils together well and store in the bottle.

Two Aromatherapy Recipes for Arthritis

There are two effective recipes for alleviating pain from arthritis. In both recipes, you will need a dark colored, airtight glass container and two fluid ounces of carrier oil. Hemp seed, jojoba and pomegranate seed are ideal carrier oils because they are known for their anti-inflammatory properties.

The essential oil blend for the first recipe would contain twenty drops of Roman Chamomile and four drops of Black Pepper. The second recipe would be a blend of ten drops pr Roman Chamomile and ten drops of Helichrysum.

Blend the carrier oil with the chosen essential oil blends, then store in the container. Gently massage a small amount of the mixture oil into the joints when suffering pain.

Aromatherapy Cure for Bruises

You will need a fluid ounce of either Jojoba Oil or Sweet Almond Oil as your carrier oil, then eight drops of Helichrysum Essential Oil. Mix the oils together in a bowl and store in a dark colored glass bottle. Apply this to a bruise in a light manner for about twice a day. As an alternative to Helichrysum, you may also opt to other oils with anti inflammatory properties such as Roman Chamomile, German Chamomile or Yarrow Essential Oil.

Aromatherapy Cure for Congestion and Sinusitis

For a natural cure for congestion, you will need a dark colored glass bottle with an orifice reducer cap and an aromatherapy inhaler. If you do not have an aromatherapy inhaler, you may use a cotton ball.For the ingredients, you will need thirty drops of eucalyptus oil, twenty six drops of Ravensara essential oil, four drops of peppermint essential oil. Blend all the oils inside the bottle.

If you are using an aromatherapy inhaler, follow the instructions on how to apply the essential oil blend to the inhaler. This is usually done by soaking the insert in the essential oil blend before putting it inside the tube. If you are using a cotton ball, pour two to three drops of the mixture and raise the cotton ball to your nose. Inhale.

Four Aromatherapy Recipes for Anxiety

These aromatherapy recipes can be used to reduce anxiety in a variety of ways. You can use a diffuser blend, in which case you have to follow the manufacturer's instructions on how to apply the aromatherapy oils to the diffuser blend. You can also convert the recipe into a bath oil by multiplying the blend by three for a total of fifteen drops as required by the bath oil recipe above; a bath salt by multiplying the blend by four to obtain the twenty drops as required by the bath salt recipe above; a massage oil by multiplying the blend by two to obtain the ten drops required by the massage oil recipe above or as an air freshener by multiplying the blend by six to obtain the thirty drops required by the air freshener recipe below.

There are four effective blends known to help reduce anxiety. The first blend contains two drops of Bergamot Essential Oil, two drops Clary Sage Essential Oil, and a drop of Frankincense Essential Oil. The second blend contains three drops of Sandalwood Essential Oil and two drops of Bergamot Essential Oil. The third blend contains three drops of Lavender Essential Oil and Clary Sage Essential Oil. And the fourth blends a drop of Rose Essential Oil, a drop of Lavender Essential Oil, a drop of Vertiver and two drops of Mandarin Essential Oil.

Four Aromatherapy Recipes for Energy and Staying Alert

These blends will help boost your energy to finish your tasks when you feel overly exhausted or fatigued. There are four effective blends for stimulating your nerves. The first one contains two drops of

Basil Essential Oil, a drop of Cypress Essential Oil, and two drops of Grapefruit Essential Oil. The second blend contains three drops of Grapefruit Essential Oil and two drops of Ginger Essential Oil. The third blend contains two drops of Rosemary Essential Oil and three drops of Bergamot Essential Oil. And the fourth blend contains a drop of Frankincense Essential Oil, two drops of Peppermint and two drops of Lemon.

To use the blends, you can use a diffuser blend, in which case you have to follow the manufacturer's instructions on how to apply the aromatherapy oils to the diffuser blend. You can also convert the recipe into a bath oil by multiplying the blend by three for a total of fifteen drops as required by the bath oil recipe above; a bath salt by multiplying the blend by four to obtain the twenty drops as required by the bath salt recipe above; a massage oil by multiplying the blend by two to obtain the ten drops required by the massage oil recipe above or as an air freshener by multiplying the blend by six to obtain the thirty drops required by the air freshener recipe below.

Nine Aromatherapy Recipes for Reducing Anger and Irritability

There are four blends of Aromatherapy Essential Oils that you can use to reduce anger. The first blend contains three drops of Orange Essential Oil, a drop of Vetiver Essential Oil, and a drop of Rose Essential Oil. The second blend contains three drops of Bergamot Essential Oil, a drop of Ylang Ylang and a drop of Jasmine Essential Oil. The third blend contains two drops of Bergamot, two drops of Orange and a drop of Roman Chamomile Essential Oil. And the fourth blend contains three drops of

Orange and two drops of Patchouli Essential Oil.

On the other hand, there are five essential oil blends that can help reduce irritability. The first blend would include three drops of Mandarin Essential Oil and two drops of Lavender Essential Oil. The second blend contains two drops of lavender Essential Oil, two drops of Roman Chamomile Essential Oil and a drop of Neroli. The third blend would include four drops of Sandalwood and a drop of Neroli. The fourth blend includes three drops of Sandalwood and two drops of Mandarin Essential Oil. And the fifth blend includes three drops of Roman Chamomile and two drops of Mandarin.

You can use these essential blends through a diffuser blend, a bath oil recipe, a bath salt recipe, a massage oil recipe or an air freshener recipe. Follow the instructions contained in the preceding recipe.

Four Aromatherapy Recipes for Depression

There are four effective essential oil recipes that are known to help one's mood during times of depression and anxiety.

The first blend would include three drops of Sandalwood Essential Oil a drop of Rose Essential Oil and a drop of Orange Essential Oil. The second blend contains two drops of Clary Sage Essential Oil and three drops of Bergamot Essential Oil. The third blend would include three drops of Grapefruit Essential Oil, a drop of Lavender and a drop of Ylang Ylang Essential Oil. And the fourth blend includes two drops of Frankincense, two drops of Jasmine and a drop of Lemon. You can use these essential blends through a diffuser blend, a bath oil recipe, a bath salt recipe, a massage oil recipe or an air freshener recipe. Follow the instructions contained in the preceding recipe.

Aromatherapy Recipe for Calming and Relaxing

To help relax and calm someone's nerves, follow this recipe and gently massage the oil mixture into his feet. A dark, airtight glass container will suffice for storage. For the ingredients, you will need a fluid ounce of carrier oil. Sweet almond is recommended. For the essential oil blend, you will need seven drops of Roman Chamomile and Lavender Essential Oil. Mix the oils together in a bowl then transfer to the glass container.

Four Aromatherapy Recipes for Stress Relief

There are four effective aromatherapy essential oil blends for stress relief. The first blend contains three drops of Clary Sage Oil, a drop of Lemon Essential Oil and a drop of Lavender Essential Oil. The second one includes two drops of Roman Chamomile Essential Oil, two drops of Lavender Oil and a drop of Vetiver Oil. The third blend comprises of three drops of Bergamot Essential Oil, a drop of Geranium Essential Oil and a drop of Frankincense. And the fourth blend contains three drops of Grapefruit Oil, a drop of Jasmine Oil and a drop of Ylang Ylang Essential Oil.

You can use these essential blends through a diffuser blend, a bath oil recipe, a bath salt recipe, a massage oil recipe or an air freshener recipe. Follow the instructions contained in the recipes above.

Chapter 14: Choosing Your Carrier Oils

The variety of carrier oils available for you to choose from as a newbie in the science of aromatherapy can get you a little bit confused at first; however, don't worry because this book will cover that.

Choosing your carrier oils is not too different from choosing your essential oils- you simply choose carrier oil that has all the properties you desire and can provide you with all the benefits you want from aromatherapy.

This means you must arm yourself with basic information about the carrier oil and its properties to help you know if it is ideal for what you wish to achieve using aromatherapy. Some properties you need to look out for include the action and viscosity of the carrier oils. You can experiment with different blends until you find a blend that suits your specific needs. This is one of the most important keys to succeeding with aromatherapy and getting the most satisfactory results. We will talk about synergy in aromatherapy later, which will focus on blending different oils to get a blend that provides more enhanced benefits.

Below are some common carrier oils used in Aromatherapy

Almond Oil

This carrier oil is perfect for dry, irritated and aging skin. It has very soothing, nourishing and skin reconditioning effects and is believed to be high in Vitamin D, proteins and GLA acids.

Apricot Kernel Oil

This carrier oil is excellent for all skin types including. It is high in vitamins A, C and E. Its light texture makes it easily absorbed into the skin.

Arnica Infused Oil

This is simply olive oil infused with Arnica. It is traditionally used as an herbal remedy for bruises, inflammation, and joint pains. It is known to act fast and gets absorbed into the skin fast. However, it is advised you do not apply it to open wounds.

Avocado Oil

This carrier oil is excellent for sensitive, irritated skin as well as for treating skin conditions such as severely dry or aged skin, psoriasis and eczema. It is deeply nourishing and soothing as well. This carrier oil contains Vitamins A, B1, B2, D and E. It also contains amino acids, panthethenic acid, lecithin, and several other essential fatty acids.

Borage Seed Oil

This carrier oil is good for aging, sunburned and damaged skin. It is one of the widely known sources of essential fatty acids, vitamins and minerals. It is good for relieving pains and excellent for supporting the mobility of tissues and joints.

There are several other carrier oils such as Coconut oil, evening primrose, GrapeSeed oil, Kukuinut oil, Jojoba oil, Neem oil, Ricebran oil, Rosehip oil, Sunflower oil, St. Johns Wort oil, Comfrey Infused Oil, Rosemary Infused Oil, Sea Buckthorn Oil, etc.

Let us look at some ideas of using carrier oil

Some ideas on how to use your carrier oil in aromatherapy

Sweet Almond, Apricot and Peach are very versatile and can be used for both facial treatments and body massages since they are easily absorbed because of their very light viscosity. If you are allergic to nuts, sunflower should be a good alternative.

Borage, Evening Primrose, Black seed, Rosehip and Jojoba oils all deliver very impressive results when used in facial aromatherapy treatments, but for body massages, you need to dilute them with much lighter oils.

Wheatgerm and unrefined Avocado are excellent for nourishing your skin when used as an overnight aromatherapeutic treatment. However, they are a bit too heavy to be used for body massages. They also have very strong odor, which some people find a bit offensive. If you can ignore their offensive odors, you can be sure to enjoy their rich nutrients and essential fatty acids that help keep your skin soft.

Let's see synergy in aromatherapy:

Synergy In Aromatherapy

Every essential oil used in aromatherapy is already a synergy of different natural ingredients with specific healing properties. This explains why aromatherapy is so effective for the treatment and cure of different ailments using these wonder oils from plants.

Each of these oils is made up of several chemical compounds; one of nature's numerous wonders one can't fathom in all totality. A single plant can contain specific compounds in different parts like the roots, stem, leaves, flower, fruits, which when combined can become a very potent formula for the cure of a myriad of diseases.

The complex structure of the chemical compounds contained in essential oils derived from plants is the reason why one essential oil can have multiple healing benefits. For instance, peppermint oil helps treat nervous, skin, hepatic, immune, circulatory, psychological and intestinal disorders.

However, the use of chemical substances such as pesticides, herbicides, germicides and chemical fertilizers can lead to loss of some of the rich phyto-chemical compounds contained in these essential oils from plant species, thereby decreasing their healing effects. This explains the need to synergize some of these oils once their components, properties and benefits are known to increase diversity in unity. Combining some of these oils to meet a specific need help create more potent complex formulae without upsetting the natural balance.

Blending tips you may find useful:

Blend different oils known to cure a particular disease for enhanced effect

Blend oils from different parts of the same plant

Blend oils that contain same active ingredients

Blend oils with same biochemical make up.

Aromatherapy Blends For Taking Care of Different Ailments

We already talked about synergy and how blending different essential oils can help you produce more impressive and lasting results. When it comes to blending your carrier oil and essential oils to meet different needs, your choice of carrier or essential oil will be determined by what health condition you are trying to manage. For every 1 fl.ounce carrier oil, add 10-12 drops of essential oils. Make sure you refer to the list of oils we mentioned eailer and choose oils that complement each other.

Blends

For stress

6 drops of Clary Sage

2 drops of Lemon

3 drops of Lavender

For improved sleep

5 drops of Lavender

5 drops of Roman Chamomile

Relief for sore muscle**s**

4 drops peppermint

2 drops of Ginger

1 drop of Black pepper

5 drops of Eucalyptus

Sex drive blend

8 drops of Sandalwood

2 drops of Jasmine

To Use

Mix the oils thoroughly and store in an airtight, dark glass container. Use ½-1 teaspoon for massage.

Aromatherapy Massage To Relieve Stress, Tension And Feel More Relaxed

The aromatherapy massage technique below can be used by anyone at home, in the work place or anywhere else. If you are using these steps at home on someone or you get someone to use them on you while at home, any flat, clean, uncluttered surface can work well as a massage table. Simply lie down or get your subject to lie face down.

Select and apply a suitable blend of essential oil and carrier oil.

Start from the legs with strokes delivered with flat palms moving in long, smooth motions starting from the ankle down to the knees or all the way up to the hip region. This helps spread the oil evenly and warms the tissues. Follow this by working on tight areas around your leg.

Repeat the same massage strokes on the back on both sides of the spine, covering the entire back region. After warming up the back tissues, use the fingers, wrists, knuckles and sometimes elbows to work more deeply on the tissues. Tight muscles can be relieved by working locally in the tight areas with firm and gentle strokes.

The arms and hands can be worked on while you or your subject lies either face down or face up. The same strokes and movements used on the legs and back region are to be repeated until all tensed muscles have been worked on and relieved of tension.

The remaining part of the massage can be done while your subject lies face down. Reach under the neck to comb your fingers upward from the back up to the base of the skull. If the patient is lying face down, allow the weight of his neck to indicate the amount of pressure you need to apply with your fingers so as not to apply too much pressure, to avoid muscle cramping or injury because of the awkward angle of the hands. Moderate intense stroking movements can be used across the top of the shoulders because that region is more prone to muscle tension. Stroke the upper chest area making sure you avoid the throat area.

For the facial area, use flat palms in gentle upward motion to stroke over the head as a way of relaxing the face. To release tensions, make gentle circular strokes from the forehead going all the way down to the chin. Use your knuckles to massage the subject's jaw line. This can be done by stroking small, light friction circles that begin from the cheeks and move outwards to the jaw joints. The light circles can equally move up to the ears and behind the ears. As the strokes gently progress to the temple region, lighter pressure should be applied. Use the pads of your thumbs to smoothen the forehead starting from between the eyebrows, while stroking in outward motion as you move to the temples.

Massage the feet last in order not to introduce bacteria from the feet to other parts of the body. You can start the feet massage from the ankles and go across the top of the foot towards the toe area with gentle strokes and moderate pressures. Roll each toe between the fingers and tug gently. Apply circular friction to the soles of the feet and heels using your thumb pads. Make sure you wash your hands after foot massages.

Chapter 15: General Uses Of Oils For Various Diseases

Basil It is an uplifting oil and relaxing also. It is generally used to dispel anxiety, Depression, Fainting, Headache, Indigestion. Influenza, General problems of menstruation, Mental Fatigue. Nausea and Pre-menstrual Syndrome etc.

Bay It is a relaxing oil and used in Arthritis, Bronchitis, body odour and Rheumatism.

Benzoin—It helps to stimulation, hence a stimulating oil. Used for Arthritis, Body odour, Bronchitis, Chills and for colds. Cystitis.

Bergamot—It is both relaxing and uplifting oil. Used mainly for Anxiety, Acne, Cystitis, Depression, Fainting and infections of throat

Cedar wood—A relaxing oil. Dispels Acne, Bronchitis, Dandruff, Eczema, Insomnia, Sexual problems.

Chamomile—It is known for relaxing. Used in Acne, Anxiety, Arthritis, Bronchitis, Dandruff, Eczema, Insomnia, Sexual problems.

Cinnamon It is also a relaxing oil. Used for low spirits. Vitality, Colds, Chills, Constipation, Depression, Diarrhoea, Influenza, Muscular aches, and Sexual problems.

Comfrev—A relaxing oil. Used in Athlete's foot, Eczema, Menopausal problems, Painful periods and Muscular aches.

Cypress— A relaxing oil. Dispels anxiety, Body odour, Cellulite, Cystitis, Depression. Diarrhoea, Eczema, Piles, Insomnia. Influenza, Menopausal problems, Painful peroiods, Mental fatigue. Obesity

(Fatness), Premenstrul Syndrome (PMS), Rheumatism, Vericose Veins, Warts Etc.

Eucalyptus—It is a stimulating oil. Used in Acne, Arthritis, Bronchitis, Chills/Colds, loose motions, cystitis, Hay fever, Headache, Influenza, Muscular aches, Rheumatism, Siniesetis, Throat infections.

Fennel—A stimulating oil, dispels constipation. Flatulence, Menopausal problems. Nausea, obesity.

Frankincense—It is a relaxing oil. Dispels colds/chills, Insomnia, Throat infections.

Geranium—It is an uplifting and relaxing oil. Used in Anxiety, Chills/colds, Dandruff, Eczema, Diarrhoea, Hormonal Regulation, Menopausal problems, Stress, Throat infections and retention of water.

Hyssop—A relaxing and stimulating oil. Used for High Blood Pressure, Bronchitis, Cellulite, Eczema, Painful periods. Sinusitis.

Jasmine—A relaxing oil. Used for anxiety, Depression, Eczema, Painful periods, Sinusitis.

Juniper—A relaxing and uplifting oil. Useful in Acne, Anxiety, Bronchitis, cystitis. Dandruff. Diarrhoea, Eczema, Flatulence, Indigestion, general menstrual problems, irregular and painful menstrual periods, mental fatigue, P.M.S., Rheumatism, vericose veins, water retention.

Lavender—Relaxing and uplifting oil. Used for Acne, Anxiety, Arthritis, Athlete's foot, hypertension, Body odour. Bronchitis, Colds, Chills, Dandruff, Depression, Diarrhoea, Fainting, Flatulence, Hay-fever, Indigestion, Insomnia, Menopausal problems, general menstrual problems, irregular periods. Muscular aches, Nausea, P.M.S., Rheumatism, Sunutitis, Stress, Throat Infections, Travel sickness, water and water retention.

Lemon—It is a stimulating oil, used for Acne, Athlete's foot, Dandruff, Diarrhoea, Fainting, Hormonal regulation, Menopausal problems. Rheumatism, Throat infections and Vericase veins.

Lemon Grass—It is also a stimulant. Used for Acne, Arthritis, Body odour. Depression, Headache, Indigestion, Rheumatism, Throat infection and Vericose veins.

Marforam—A relaxing oil, used to dispel anxiety, Arthritis, Hypertension, Body odour, constipation, Headache, Indigestion, Insomnia, Painful periods, Muscular aches, Rheumatism and stress.

Melissa—An uplifting and relaxing oil. Cures Anxiety, Hypertension, Diarrhoea, Piles, Headache, Indigestion, Menopausal problems, general menstrual problems. Irregular periods. Painful periods, Mental fatigue, Nausea, PMS and Stress.

Myrrh—It is a stimulating oil. Used for Bronchitis, chills/colds, Diarrhoea, Eczema, Flatulence, Hormonal regulation and Throat infections.

Neroli —A relaxing oil. Used for anxiety, Body ache, Depression. Insomnia, Problems of Menopause, PMS, Rheumatism, Sexual problems.

Orange—An uplifting oil. Used to treat anxiety. Hypertension, constipation, Depression, Hormonal regulation and Menopausal problems.

Parsley—A stimulating oil. Used to dispel constipation, Depression, Hormonal regularities, Indigestion, Menopausal Problems.

Patchouli—A relaxing oil. Used to dispel Acne, Anxiety, Arthritis, Bronchitis, Dandruff, Depression, Eczema, Obesity, Sexual Problems.

Peppermint—It is a stimulating oil. Used to treat hypertension. Body odour, Bronchitis, Diarrhoea, Fainting, Flatulence, Piles, Headache, Indigestion, Nausea, Stress, Vericose, Veins and Warts.

Pine—A stimulating oil. Used for Arthritits, Body ache. Body odour,.Colds, Chills, Cystitis, Influenza, Mental fatigue. Muscular aches, Rheumatism, Sinusitis, water retention.

Rose—It is a relaxing oil. Useful for anxiety, Arthritis, Cellulite, Dandruff, Depression, Hay fever, Insomnia, General Menopausal problems, Painful and irregular periods, Mental fatigue, Muscular aches, Rheumatism, Sinusitis, water retention.

Rosemary—A stimulating oil. Used for Hypertension, Bronchitis, Chills/colds, Constipation, Depression, Piles, Insomnia, Menupausal problems. Painful and irregular periods, Nausea, PMS and Sexual problems.

Sage—A stimulating oil. Used in anxiety, Arthrit, low B.P., Body ache. Cystitis, Dandruff, Depression, Fainting, Flatulence, Headache, Indigestion, Menstrual problems, Irregular periods, Mental fatigue, Muscular aches, Obesity, PMS, Rheumatism, Travel Sickness, Water Retention.

Cary sage—It is Stimulating and Relaxing oil. Used in Anxiety, High Blood Pressure, Depression, Flatulence, Insomnia, Menopausal Problems, Irregular and Painful periods. Mental fatigue, PMS, Sexual problems, Throat infections.

Sandal wood—It is a relaxing oil. Used in Acne, Anxiety, Body odour. Cystitis, Dandruff, Diarrhoea, Depression, Eczema, Piles, Insomnia, Nausea, PMS, Sexual Problems, Stress, Throat infections.

Tea Tree—Used in Athelete's Foot, Bronchitis, Colds, chills, Depression, Influenza, Throat Infections, Warts.

Thyme—It is a stimulating oil. Used to dispel anxiety, Bronchitis, Cold/chills, Flatulence, Menstrual Problems, Mental fatigue, Obesity, Pre-menstrual Syndrome (PMS), Rheumatism.

Ylang-Ylang—It is a relaxing oil. Used to dispel anxiety. Hypertension, Depression and sexual problems.

Keynotes

The above mentioned diseases, covered under one type of essential oil also are the leading symptoms of maladies but it does also imply that a subject oil is capable of curing other (minor) maladies also. In any case always seek help of a qualified and experienced aromatherapist for proper guidance on use of any oil and also which carrier oil will be best suited as a vehicle for blending.

Persons, having highly sensitive skin and olfactory nerver, find some of the oils not suiting them, causing skin related and breathing reactions. Further, not more than three oils should ever be blended, in case of a single treatment, because synergesic effects cannot be predicted off hand.

Normally a dilution is prepared by adding 10 drops of essential oil to 20 ml. quantity of carrier oil. If more than one oil is to be added, the quantity and ratio of essential oil should be proportionately reduced. In case of sensitive skin, babies, pregnant ladies, prepare a low dilution of 5 drops to 20 ml. of carrier oil.

Pregnancy

In pregnancy never use Basil, Bay, Cary sage, Comfrey, Marforam, Mellisa. Myrrh. Rosemarry, Sage and Thyne during pregnancy, and consult an aromatherapist about suitability of particular oil, in case of pregnancy, due to reaction factor.

Main Essential Oils and Cautions

German Chamovile—It is anti-allergic, anti-inflammatory, antispasmodic and sedative and should not be used during pregnancy due to its capability of causing dermatites in some patients.

Clary Sage—It has analgesic, sedative, and anti-spasmodic qualities. Avoidance of alcohol before and after use of this oil is imperative. It may be used to promote labour pain but must not be used during pregnancy.

Peppermint—It is Carminative, antiseptic and antis-pasmodic oil and must not be used for children below 12 years of age. Use it low dilution. Further, it should not be used before, during and after any homeopathic treatment, as it takes away effect of homeopathic medicines due to its strong smell.

Conclusion

As should be obvious, there are numerous advantages related with the utilization of fundamental oils and fragrant healing. Basic oils have been utilized since forever for corrective, otherworldly, and enthusiastic reasons. The utilization of these oils have guided a huge number of individuals to an absolutely all-encompassing feeling of health and, ideally, this digital book has begun you along the way too.

Fragrant healing is a flexible type of reciprocal medication and furthermore one that is extremely simple to use from various perspectives to treat an assortment of physical, passionate, and otherworldly illnesses.

Different fragrances trigger various sensations and feelings in various individuals and one of the numerous advantages of fragrant healing is the straightforwardness with which you can tailor your treatment to your particular needs.

Regardless of whether it be by means of packs, sweet-smelling back rub, inward breath, or some other strategy for application, the remedial properties of basic oils can transform yourself to improve things. These advantages, in mix with regular medication, can assume a noticeable function in keeping up your overall wellbeing and prosperity.

I urge you to keep searching out different assets on fragrance based treatment and basic oils so as to all the more likely tailor the aromas you use to help in your recuperating. Don't hesitate to explore different avenues regarding the plans gave to customize your fragrance based treatment experience.

As you proceed with your training on the utilization of fundamental oils and the investigation of fragrance based treatment, consistently recollect that if all else fails; counsel your medical care supplier or an enrolled aromatherapist to guarantee that you have the most complete and exact data accessible.

www.ingramcontent.com/pod-product-compliance
Lightning Source LLC
Chambersburg PA
CBHW060322030426
42336CB00011B/1161